CAROLINA BEACH MUSIC

THE CLASSIC YEARS

RICK SIMMONS

Charleston · London

THE
History
PRESS

Published by The History Press
Charleston, SC 29403
www.historypress.net

Front cover: top, left to right: courtesy of Clifford Curry; courtesy of Gary Barker; bottom, left to right: courtesy of the North Carolina Office of Archives and History, Raleigh, North Carolina; courtesy of Bobby and John Tomlinson.
Back cover, top to bottom: courtesy of Bob Kuban; courtesy of Donald Hobson; courtesy of Sandra Peoples Bears and Beverly Johnson; courtesy of John McElrath.

First published 2011

ISBN 978-1-5402-0571-1

Library of Congress Cataloging-in-Publication Data
Simmons, Rick.
Carolina beach music : the classic years / Rick Simmons.
p. cm.
ISBN 978-1-5402-0571-1
1. Popular music--North Carolina--History and criticism. 2. Popular music--South Carolina--History and criticism. 3. Musicians--North Carolina. 4. Musicians--South Carolina. 5. Musical groups--North Carolina. 6. Musical groups--South Carolina. 7. Shag (Dance)--History. I. Title.
ML3411.5.S56 2011
781.6409757'0904--dc22
2011006268

CONTENTS

Contents

CONTENTS

CONTENTS

CONTENTS

CONTENTS

ACKNOWLEDGEMENTS

When I started this project, I knew that unless I offered some type of personal insight into the songs by the artists, it would be just another book about music. Although many of the artists who sang these songs have passed away, I was still able to track down a number of them, though often with great difficulty. I think I've covered everyone I interviewed in the list below, as well as the people who sent and sometimes took the great pictures the artists provided and helped me schedule interviews, find source materials or anything else. I have endeavored to be as accurate as possible in anything found within this book, and if something is incorrect I apologize. To all I say thanks.

Of the featured artists and performers I talked to, I wish to thank Gary Barker of the Catalinas, Sandra Peoples Bears of the Jewels, Jan Bradley, Norm Burnett of the Tymes, G.C. Cameron of the Spinners, Bruce Channel, Paul Craver of Cannonball, Clifford Curry, Clem Curtis of the Foundations, Hershey Deville of Jewell and the Rubies, Earl Gardner of the Coasters, Donald Hobson of Gene Barbour and the Cavaliers, James Holvay and Al Herrera of the MOB, Linda "Quig" Quinlan James of the Monzas, Bob Kuban of Bob Kuban and the In-Men, Meadowlark Lemon of the Globetrotters, Gene McDaniels, John McElrath of the Swingin' Medallions, Bobby Moore Jr. of Bobby Moore and the Rhythm Aces, Deacon John Moore, Freda Payne, Wayne Pittman of the O'Kaysions, Charles Pope of the Tams, Billy Scott of the Georgia Prophets, Ammon Tharp of Bill Deal & the Rhondels, Sonny Threatt of Sunny and Phyllis, Bobby Tomlinson of the Embers, Sonny Turner of the Platters, Pat Upton of the Spiral Starecase and Brenton Wood. I'd also like to thank those individuals who, while perhaps not performers on the songs, did help me get the interviews or pictures, offered insight or helped with research: Bob Abrahamian, Joe Accardi, Johnnie Allen, Charlie Brown (Ed Weiss), Steve Cantor, Marion Carter, Edward Cermanski, Consuelo Curtis, Randy Floyd, Kenny Futch, Veta Gardner, Charlie Horner, Beverly Johnson, Candy Kaye, Ken Knox, Mark Layne, Cara Lee, Sam Lollar, Christine McMeans, Don Peake, Dianne Pope, David Rachou, Todd Richard, Al Schrank, Jackie Stander, John Tomlinson and Richard Younger. Also, a special thanks to those longtime friends who let me bounce ideas off of them or helped me get information: Dennis Abbott, Charlie Aiken, Steve Bond, Chappy Chapman, Steve Cline, Ronnie Critz, Bob Dunn, Kirk Edmonds, Richard Harvin, Len Hutchison, Jimmy Isom, Hank Mabry, Bob Mundy, Milton Pate, Dan Patillo, Phil Payne, Chris Pearce, Hall Province, Tim Reed, Rush Smith, Forest Suggs and Matt Ward. A *really* big thanks to Ricky Saucier and Woody Lynch, who helped me find and contact several of these artists, and for his help (again) with pictures, Warren Cockfield. Finally, to Sue, Courtenay, Cord, Julie and Dad. Without you, there'd be no book. My heartfelt thanks.

INTRODUCTION

G rowing up in South Carolina, I knew what beach music was, though admittedly at first my knowledge wasn't that extensive. Early on I associated beach music with the Tams, Drifters, Platters and a few other groups and knew that beach music was *not* California surf music. But beyond that, I didn't know a whole lot other than that I liked the sound. But as time went on, and into my high school years, I started to really love it and came to understand that music by artists such as Brenton Wood, the Showmen, Willie Tee, Arthur Alexander, Clifford Curry and others was also considered beach music. Regarding these classic R&B acts as beach groups made me a bit of a purist, and I came to the conclusion that beach music should principally be '50s and '60s rhythm and blues. I broadened my horizons a bit when I entered Clemson University in the fall of 1976 and joined the Kappa Alpha Order, and many of the bands we booked for KA parties, like the Catalinas, Georgia Prophets and Embers, were also considered beach bands, though they played some of their own music and some of it was not-so-old.

But to reconsider for a moment, why is any of this music considered "beach music" in the Carolinas? Donald Hobson of Gene Barbour and the Cavaliers has an interesting theory about how songs like those in this book, though not recorded to be beach music, *became* beach music in the Carolinas. He notes that during the '60s, his band, like many other regional bands, would play down at the beach a lot, and "we played a lot of the music that kids danced to in the more popular jukebox joints such as The Pad and The Salty Dog." A lot of that was music that national groups like the Tams, the Drifters, the Showmen, the Platters and others played, and those groups became popular in the Carolinas, and especially at the beaches, "because they were 'affordable' national recording artists." While large venues in places like Raleigh, Columbia and Charlotte "could afford the really big-name artists like James Brown, the Four Tops and Stevie Wonder, the smaller venues could not." So groups that perhaps had recorded only a few hits, or that, perhaps, had been off the charts for a few years "found a regular comfort zone in the Carolinas' dance clubs" and especially where there were a lot of clubs—at the beaches.

As a result, this danceable music became associated with the beach, but what really cemented the whole "beach music" thing in the Carolinas? Hobson believes that by the late '60s and early '70s, it was becoming more difficult for bands to play covers of then-current Top 40 tunes, as the music was becoming more and more elaborate or often had a harder edge and was not danceable. Rather than adding a horn section, or perhaps changing their sound completely, some bands chose instead to stick with the older songs. "You'd go hear a band and they wouldn't be playing Top 40 at all… but would be pulling out those old jukebox tunes such as 'Thank You John,' 'My Girl,' '39-21-40 Shape,' 'Sixty-Minute Man'…In a nutshell, they played the old music—*the music we used to hear down at the beach*—and the term 'beach music' seemed to catch hold." Consequently, Hobson says, though his bands played all of those songs we now call beach music, the term itself was a retronym, because when they played it originally, it wasn't *yet* beach music. Many of the artists I interviewed agreed and noted that the term "beach music" gradually came to be used during the late '60s and really took its irrevocable hold by the early '70s. At the same time, since the shag was the dance best suited for those very danceable songs played in those beach clubs, early '70s songs that were also "shaggable" came under the umbrella of beach music as well, creating a solid body of what we'd now call "classic" Carolina beach music by the early 1970s.

While this doesn't fully explain the whole beach music phenomenon (I'm not sure any explanation can), it's a good start. Because this music has been such an important part of my life for so many years, after three previous books about matters more academic, I decided I wanted to write a book about classic beach music. I decided my book would focus on the songs—how and if they charted on the Billboard charts in mainstream America, the songs' origins and so on—the stories behind the music, if you will. As a result, what you see before you is the result of the formative influence of warm summer nights, fraternity parties and the pleasure of listening to great music.

HOW AND WHY I CHOSE *THESE* SONGS

In this book, my goal was to discuss songs that most people would consider indisputable beach classics, but of course there's always room for discussion. Generally, beach music is also about dancing, but it's hard to mandate that a great beach song has to be one that is ideal for shagging. By that standard, uptempo songs such as "Double Shot" and "More Today than Yesterday" might not be such good beach songs, but good beach songs they are. Consequently, I didn't limit myself only to good shag songs.

The next step was to define my parameters, and this where I had to make a difficult decision. In my mind, the Catalinas' "Summertime's Calling Me" was an important signpost in the road. After this song became popular in the Carolinas, beach music started to become self-aware, and from that point on more and more songs started to be created to *be* beach music. Before that, songs like the ones in this book were recorded to get national airtime, to sell records and hopefully to make the Top 40, not simply to fit a niche market. I wanted the focus of this book to be mainly songs that were national releases that were adopted as Carolina beach music, and to that end, all but three of the songs in this book received national distribution. Because of the separation that occurred in the mid-1970s, I decided to make this survey end the year that "Summertime's Calling Me" came out—1975. That gave me roughly thirty years of classic beach music to work with, even though I had to omit some fantastic post-1975 songs. However, you have to draw the line somewhere, and I'll leave the post-1975 years for another time.

That left only the song selection, which was the hardest part. To come up with the 100 most essential songs, I asked friends, read Top 100 lists, collated song lists on beach music anthologies and basically compiled every bit of information I could about people's favorite beach music songs. I think most people will agree that the majority of the big-time classic beach tunes are covered here, but I am also fully aware that I can (and have) come up with another list of 100 songs that would be just as powerful. Nevertheless, difficult decisions and all, authoring this book has been the most enjoyable writing experience I've ever had.

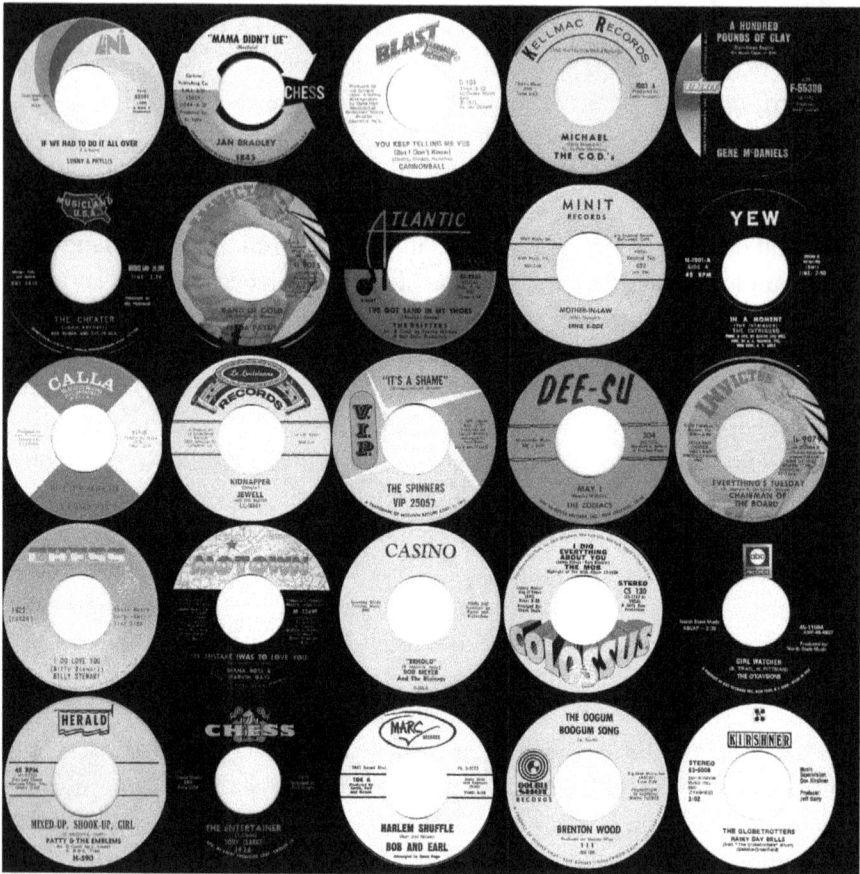

ARTHUR ALEXANDER

"You Better Move On"
1962, Billboard #24
Dot 16309

"Anna"
1962, Billboard #68
Dot 16387

"Arthur was an erratic person," Arthur Alexander's biographer, Richard Younger, told me, and like many people who knew him, Younger saw that Alexander's idiosyncratic behavior could be hard to explain and "open to any interpretation." Perhaps this helps explain the long fall Alexander took from writing and recording Top 100 hits like "Anna" and "You Better Move On" and having the Beatles and Rolling Stones cover them to becoming a janitor and part-time bus driver living in anonymity. But the music business can be harsh and unforgiving, even for those who make it big—and Alexander *was* big. His work inspired more cover versions by more famous singers and groups than the work of any other artist with a beach music hit, and recordings of his songs were not only done by the Beatles and Rolling Stones but also by Bob Dylan and Elvis Presley, which puts him in elite company indeed. And although personal issues became almost debilitating and led to Alexander leaving the music business altogether, his music has endeared him to beach music fans for decades.

Even as a teenager living near Muscle Shoals, Alabama, it was apparent that Arthur Alexander had a very special gift. His first success was when he co-wrote a song called "She Wanna Rock," which was recorded by Amie Derkson in 1959, and he also co-wrote "Sally Sue Brown," which he recorded in 1960 and which would later be recorded by Bob Dylan. According to Younger, by then Alexander was married, a father and working part time as a bellhop and selling bootleg liquor to make ends meet. It was at this point he wrote another song that would become his second recording, "You Better Move On," and when it was released in 1962, the record finally brought him some notice. The first of many songs he would record chronicling problematic relationships, the song was based on his early relationship with his girlfriend (who would become his wife) Ann, and how her former boyfriend, who was from a wealthy family, tried to win her back. "I know you can buy her fancy clothes and diamond rings," Alexander says, but "you better move on." The song went to #24 on the charts, Alexander appeared on *American Bandstand* and suddenly he was on his way. In later years, the soulful side would be covered by the Rolling Stones, the Hollies and Chuck Jackson, among others.

After another release, his next recording was 1962's "Anna," written about Ann and their doomed relationship, which would ultimately end in divorce. Its title doesn't match the lyrics, as the full title of the record is "Anna (Go to Him)," though Alexander repeatedly sings, "go *with* him." "With" or "to" didn't make much difference to Alexander, who later told Younger that in reality while his wife had not been unfaithful, he believed she was starting to regret not going with that other guy who had "moved on." This mournful song, which went to #68 on the pop charts, really impressed John Lennon, and as a result the Beatles recorded and released their own version on the album *Please Please Me*. The Beatles would eventually cover three other Alexander recordings, "A Shot of Rhythm and Blues," "Where Have You Been" and "Soldier of Love," and in fact, Paul McCartney later said in an interview, "If the Beatles ever wanted a sound, it was R&B...we wanted to be like Arthur Alexander."

Many groups would cover songs Alexander recorded and/or wrote, and songs such as "Burning Love" by Elvis Presley, "Sharing the Night Together" by Dr. Hook and the Medicine Show and "Everyday I Have to Cry Some" by Steve Alaimo would all do well. But on a personal level, Alexander's behavior was becoming increasingly erratic. For example, once for no apparent reason he walked offstage in the middle of a performance. Seemingly plagued by indecision about whether he wanted a career in music, not long after his own version of "Everyday I Have to Cry Some" went to #45 in 1975, he simply dropped out of sight. His friend Clifford Curry says, "I don't think Arthur ever really embraced his fame, and I think that's why he dropped out of the business and just disappeared. I think he was in awe of his success, but he just couldn't

Arthur Alexander. *Courtesy of Richard Younger.*

handle it." After quitting the business, Alexander moved to Cleveland and spent most of the rest of his life working as a bus driver and janitor. Younger told me that, surprisingly, "the people he worked with really didn't know of Arthur's previous career until the early '90s—he only told his co-workers" in 1993, when he recorded his comeback album, *Lonely Like Me*. Shortly thereafter, he suffered a fatal heart attack and died at the age of fifty-three.

Younger noted that Keith Richards of the Rolling Stones said, "When the Beatles and the Stones got their first chances to record, one did 'Anna,' and the other did 'You Better Move On.' That should tell you enough." Clearly one would have to consider Alexander a great singer and songwriter, but considering his many contributions to his own catalogue as well songs he wrote and/or recorded and others covered, it isn't hard to see that he was an underappreciated genius often laboring in relative obscurity. But Curry knows that despite his erratic behavior, Alexander knew one place he was really appreciated. "In the late '60s we did a few gigs together in the Carolinas, and he'd never even heard of beach music. He wasn't used to the beach scene, and he was trying to get a handle on what beach music was all about because he really had no idea. But he learned his records were still popular in the Carolinas and that people wanted to see him—and he was really pleased by that." Arthur Alexander's music has continued to please beach music fans ever since.

THE ARTISTICS

"I'M GONNA MISS YOU"
1966, Billboard #55
Brunswick 55301

One of the most beautiful and harmonious of all beach music songs, "I'm Gonna Miss You" was recorded by the Artistics, a group whose lineup and cohesiveness was anything but harmonious. Formed in Chicago in 1958, Aaron Floyd, Curt Thomas, Laurence Johnson and Jesse Bolian made up the original Artistics, and though they did sing at the Democratic National Convention in 1960, their success was otherwise fairly limited and local. Having now been joined by new lead vocalist Robert Dobyne, they came to the attention of Major Lance, who in 1962 had signed with Okeh records as a solo act. For Major Lance's second recording on Okeh in August 1963, he enlisted the Artistics as backup singers on "The Monkey Time," which shot up the Billboard charts to #8.

The Artistics' first taste of success, even if technically not their own, was not to be fruitless. Okeh recognized their potential and signed them to a contract, where they recorded "I Need Your Love" in 1963 before problems within the group forced Dobyne out and Charles Davis took over in his place. Even before the group laid down its next single, Davis was out and Marvin Smith, a former member of the El Dorados, was in. He took over the lead for "Get My Hands On Some Lovin,'" which was recorded in January 1964.

It wasn't only the group that was experiencing upheaval, however, but Okeh records as well. After a few more Artistics' recordings in 1965 and 1966, internal struggles at Okeh resulted in several artists leaving the label and going to Brunswick, including the Artistics. The change seemed to be the charm, as their first recording was the Marvin Smith–led "I'm Gonna Miss You." Though not a big chart hit—it only climbed to #55—it was nevertheless a step in the right direction, and at long last the Artistics seemed about to get their due.

But yet again, changes in the lineup would affect the group's continuity. Smith left for a solo career in 1967 and had in fact already recorded the solo effort "Time Stopped" backed by the Artistics in 1966. Tommy Green now came onboard as the lead vocalist, and Bernard Reed also joined the group, and for the first time in years the group had stability. This lineup of Artistics recorded a series of quality tracks for Brunswick over the next five years before they disbanded in 1973.

Perhaps because of the fluidity of the lineup, the group was never again able to match the magic that came together on "I'm Gonna Miss You." One of the most heartfelt songs in the annals of beach music, it makes one wonder what the Artistics might have done if they had been able to produce more than just one record with the Marvin Smith–led Brunswick recording lineup. Clearly their one effort under those conditions is a beach music classic.

DARRELL BANKS

"OPEN THE DOOR TO YOUR HEART"
1966, Billboard #27
Revilot 201

O nce you've heard the classic tune "Open the Door to Your Heart," you have to wonder why you haven't heard anything else by Darrell Banks. It's a powerful song, and his great voice is obviously not the type that lends itself to one-hit wonders. But Banks was in many ways his own worst enemy, and after recording just seven singles, his proclivity for conflict led to him making the mistake of pulling a gun on a police officer, who shot him dead in the street.

Banks grew up in Buffalo, New York, and like many young men who sang R&B in the 1950s and '60s, he got his start singing with gospel groups before he turned his talents to solo musical pursuits. He would often play at the Revilot Lounge in Buffalo, and there his friend Donnie Elbert wrote a song for him called "Baby Walk Right In"—the actual working title of "Open the Door to Your Heart." The song would take Banks off the lounge circuit and put him in a studio in Detroit to record the song, which went all the way to #27 on the Billboard Hot 100 and to #2 in the R&B listings. Suddenly, Banks was a hot singing commodity and Elbert had written a hit song. The two boys from Buffalo had made it big.

But apparently only *one* boy from Buffalo had made it big. When the record came out, Elbert noticed that Banks, and not he, was credited with writing the song. Willing to give Banks the benefit of the doubt, Elbert attempted to correct what he assumed was a clerical error and set right that he had written the song. Instead, he was shocked to learn that the song's rights had been given to Banks not because of an error but because Banks had told the record company (and indeed had filled out documents saying) that he alone had written the song. After a protracted legal battle, Elbert was at last able to get himself listed as co-songwriter but only as a co-writer because apparently Banks had made some minor changes, such as speeding up the tempo, so Banks was given 50 percent authorship. Perhaps it's indicative of the injustice of Banks's perfidy that while Elbert would go on to write well more than one hundred songs, "Open the Door to Your Heart" is the only song Banks would ever receive a songwriting credit for. Unfortunately, Banks's questionable behavior in this instance was a sign of things to come.

Banks stayed with Revilot for one more single, "Somebody (Somewhere) Needs You," which hit #55 that same year. Banks moved to Atco and then Cotillion, where none of his releases would chart. Nevertheless, Stax records apparently thought he still had some gas left in the tank and signed him on for a couple of singles to its Volt subsidiary, though chart success would elude him there as well. Later, an unhappy Banks had a falling out with the record company over an accidental release of a song that was credited to him, and though he had recorded *a* version of the song, it wasn't *the* version on the compilation album that Stax released.

Thus, by 1970 Banks had been involved in more than one disagreement about his music, and his tendency to find trouble boiled over into his personal life as well. Waiting at his estranged girlfriend's house one afternoon in February 1970, he saw her return home in the company of another man. An infuriated Banks pulled a gun on the man, despite the fact that he identified himself as off-duty policeman Aaron Bullock. Faced with being shot himself, Bullock shot Banks in the neck and the chest; he was declared dead at the hospital at the age of thirty-two.

After four short turbulent years and just seven singles, Darrell Banks's career was over. Banks never seemed to care much about making friends, and he let his quick temper and self-centeredness make his decisions for him. Despite his shortcomings as an individual, no one would dispute his talent or the power of the fine track "Open the Door to Your Heart."

GENE BARBOUR & THE CAVALIERS

"I NEED A LOVE"
1966, did not chart
Hit 101

"The story behind the name of the 45 is a little vague," Donald Hobson admitted when I asked why the Cavaliers had recorded the Impressions "I Need You" as "I Need a Love"—even though, as he noted, "it was a direct interpretation of the original, including all vocal parts and orchestration, and the line 'I need a love' is not even present in the lyrics." But after our interview, Hobson himself wanted to know why they'd recorded the Impressions song under a different name, and it would ultimately lead to his clearing up a forty-five-year-old mystery. Mystery and confusion aside, "I Need a Love" by Gene Barbour and the Cavaliers is perhaps the finest song not to receive national distribution recorded by a band from the Carolinas during the 1960s. In fact, in terms of its energy and passion, it far surpasses the song it covered—and many other songs we now call Carolina beach music as well.

The band started as simply the Cavaliers, and when they got together in 1963, they were Charles Aycock, Walt Jones, Paul Mattox and Donald Hobson, all of whom were in the band at Dunn High School in Dunn, North Carolina. The band started out like many others, playing high school gigs whenever they could get them. Feeling that with a little direction they could improve their sound and bookings, Hobson said, "We were fortunate to engage Walt's uncle Harry Driver as our manager." Driver brought in Tommy Ralph to play bass, and with Aycock singing lead, the group became a successful local act.

Gene Barbour and the
Cavaliers. *Courtesy of
Donald Hobson.*

But Driver was "urging us to bring on a dedicated lead singer," and it was
Aycock himself who found Gene Barbour, who had his own group called
Gene Barbour & the Shakedowns. "Gene was a good lead with a pure voice
and extreme range, and a local following of his own. Harry recognized that
if we joined forces, we could benefit from both Gene's name and our own
following. From that point, we were validated as a viable, regional R&B
cover band," Hobson says. Soon Billy Wellons joined the band and added
yet another dimension: "Billy was a great dancer in his own right, and Gene
and Billy played off each other nightly and the young girls would crowd the
stage to see those two gyrate their stuff!"

Soon Driver had the group record a song Mattox and Barbour had
co-written titled "Nobody." Though the record is now a collector's item,
Hobson says the original recording only sold "probably a 100 or so units…
we couldn't give those things away, and for months thereafter we would sail
them like Frisbees at road signs along the highway as we traveled to and from
gigs. Today, none of us has a copy, and they're worth a mint." Nevertheless,
in the summer of 1966, Driver decided to take them to Bill Lowery's studio
in Atlanta to record once again, and since "we didn't have any material of

our own, we went into the sessions and came out with covers such as 'I Dig You Baby' by Jerry Butler and 'Just Ask the Lonely' by the Four Tops," as well as that mysteriously titled 'I Need a Love.'" Produced by Ted Hall's Charlotte-based *Hit Attractions*, until our interview even Hobson thought that the song, which the Impressions had released as the single "I Need You" in 1965 (Billboard #64), was retitled by the Cavaliers management for some unknown reason. But after our first interview, Hobson started looking into it and discovered something quite interesting. After the release of their single "I Need You," the Impressions released their 1966 LP "Ridin High," which contains the exact song that charted *except* that on the LP it had a new title—"I Need a Love." This is the song that Hobson's group would record—word for word, title and all—in 1967. Hobson speculates that maybe "whoever was inputting the data and setting the type for the '66 cover and disc label layouts picked up a similar name off a list of recorded tracks, transferred the wrong name and no one caught it before it went to press." As a result, the mistake was on the Impressions album—and who

Gene Barbour and the Cavaliers perform at the IFC Dance, Township Auditorium in Columbia, South Carolina, 1966. *Courtesy of Donald Hobson.*

were the boys from Dunn to question what the Impressions themselves had seemingly named their own song? But to further complicate matters, the Impressions would in fact release yet another song with the title "I Need a Love" in 1969, which was completely different from the song the Cavaliers recorded. Hobson thinks maybe there was a song recorded in 1965 called "I Need a Love," and the album states that title, but the track for "I Need You" is what appears on the album. Hobson says it would be "interesting to know when the '69 'I Need a Love' was actually recorded. I'd bet money it was recorded at that earlier time."

As for the Cavaliers' version, it "sold pretty well regionally but nothing really significant," Hobson said. The group, however, had become one of the most popular bands in the Carolinas and played with and opened for groups including the Four Tops, Martha & the Vandellas, the Platters and Smokey Robinson & the Miracles. Yet despite their success, like many groups performing in the late 1960s, several members of the group were eventually drafted or enlisted. By the early 1970s, the Gene Barbour & the Cavaliers group that had recorded "I Need a Love" was no more.

The group "all came back together to perform through the '70s as the original Men of Distinction," Hobson said, but they never cut a song with the staying power that "I Need a Love" has had. And as for that song title? "Well, the riddle of why we released a tune with the wrong title is solved," he said. "According to the album cut, it was the *right* title." After more than four decades, it appears the question has finally been answered.

BOB AND EARL

"HARLEM SHUFFLE"
1964, Billboard #44
Marc 104

Harlem Shuffle" isn't your typical beach song; it isn't about sun, sand, girls, love or even the events of day-to-day life. It's about a dance, and not shagging, so it's really an oddity. While in the late '50s and early '60s songs about the twist, the swim, the jerk and other dances were all the rage, those aren't the types of songs that became beach music favorites. In that sense, Bob and Earl's "Harlem Shuffle" beat overwhelming odds.

Initially, Bob and Earl were former Hollywood Flames members Bobby Byrd and Earl Nelson, whose group had taken their single "Buzz Buzz Buzz" to #11 on the pop charts in 1957. Both Byrd and Nelson were interested in breaking out, and in fact earlier that year Byrd had recorded as Bobby Day and had had some chart action with "Little Bitty Pretty One," which Nelson sang backup on, and which Thurston Harris would take to #6 later in 1957. Despite the fact that his own version misfired, he would write other successful songs, such as "Over and Over," for the Dave Clark Five (#1, 1965), and his own "Rockin Robin" (#2, 1958). In 1960, he teamed up with Nelson to form the initial pairing of Bob and Earl, but by 1962 Day decided to go solo again, so Bobby Relf joined Nelson. Relf had been a member of several moderately successful groups, and one contribution he made to the new duo was that he brought along a young keyboard player named Barry White.

The first record by the new incarnation of Bob and Earl would be a local hit in Los Angeles, but their second release, "Harlem Shuffle," recorded on the fledgling Marc label, went national. Relf and Nelson co-wrote the song while loosely adapting a song called "Slauson Shuffletime" by Round Robin, and the song was about a street in L.A. But in order to make it nationally appealing, they changed to locale to the better-known Harlem area of New York, and with Bob and Earl singing the revamped tune and with White on keyboards, it went to #44 in 1964.

While the group would record other singles, their biggest subsequent hit would be "Baby It's Over," which went to #26 in 1966. Again, however, limited success led to the group's breakup, so Nelson started singing as Jackie Lee and had his own dance-based hit, "The Duck," in 1965. Relf, meantime, began recording as Bobby Garrett and saw some success as well. Then, in 1969, "Harlem Shuffle" became a hit all over again when released in England; in fact, it outdistanced its American release by climbing to #7 on the charts. Sensing an opportunity that had largely eluded them for several years, Relf and Nelson re-teamed once again as Bob and Earl to tour.

The reunion was short-lived, however, and by the early 1970s they had gone their separate ways again. Relf went back to working with Barry White (and wrote "Bring Back My Yesterdays" for him in 1973) and produced for the Love Unlimited Orchestra and Gloria Scott as well. Nelson continued to tour and record throughout the '70s and '80s. Yet despite the ever-changing and transitory nature of the duo, the song "Harlem Shuffle" would surpass anyone's expectations and would be covered by groups as diverse as Booker T and the MGs, John Fred and his Playboy Band and, most famously, the Rolling Stones, who took it all the way to #5 in 1986. The group House of Pain sampled the song on their #3 single "Jump Around" in 1993, and George Harrison claimed that Bob and Earl's version of "Harlem Shuffle" was his favorite all-time song. The British newspaper the *Daily Telegraph* ranked the song #23 on its list of the top fifty duets ever recorded.

Consequently, "Harlem Shuffle" is everything a beach music hit shouldn't be: it's a dance song, a song often recorded by rock acts and a song that's even sampled long after the golden age of beach music. Nevertheless, it remains a Carolina beach music favorite.

JAN BRADLEY

"MAMA DIDN'T LIE"
1963, Billboard #14
Chess 1845

D o I miss the music business? Sometimes I do, sometimes I don't," Jan
Bradley told the author. "It's always there," she said, "and because that's
your first love, you start thinking about how much you enjoyed it. But overall,
if I had to say one way or the other, I don't miss it. Music is moving, it's
soothing, it means a lot to most people. So it still has a big place in my life—
but I don't miss the business." Because Jan Bradley knew how to prioritize
what was important in her life, when she felt it was the right time she simply
walked away from the music industry. Before she did, she recorded some
high-quality songs, including "Mama Didn't Lie," a beach music classic.

When in high school in Chicago, Bradley was discovered at a talent show
by producer Don Talty, but because she was a minor, her parents insisted she
finish school before attempting to embark on a career in music. When Talty
finally had the opportunity to work with her, he was able to get Curtis Mayfield
of the Impressions to give her a few songs to try out. "The first Curtis Mayfield
song I did was 'We Girls,'" Bradley said, which was released on Talty's Formal
records in 1962. Though the song did well regionally and "it got me started,
got my name out there and got a lot of crossover airplay at that time," it wasn't
picked up nationally. "Next we recorded 'Mama Didn't Lie' in an effort to
continue launching my career," and this time everything clicked.

"Mama Didn't Lie" was also written by Mayfield. He had taken the song
to Bradley, and she recalls that he said, "'Okay, this is what I've got that I

think will work for you. Take a listen.' I heard 'Mama Didn't Lie' and I thought, 'I love his style, I can do this, I really like this!' When 'Mama Didn't Lie' came around and started getting airplay, it got a lot of interest from major record companies, and Chess pursued us too. We had tried to get them interested in 'We Girls' because they were a big label here in Chicago, and they specialized in R&B. Though they had passed on 'We Girls,' they wanted 'Mama Didn't Lie' and took it. The national promotion they were able to provide made it a really big hit."

"Mama Didn't Lie" was a smash, going all the way to #14 on the Billboard charts and #8 on the R&B charts in 1963. It seemed that Mayfield's writing and Bradley's voice was the magic combination for her success, and the future looked bright indeed. But then big business stepped in. "Curtis had his goals in mind for his songwriting and publishing career, and Chess wanted something he wasn't willing to part with—the rights to his music." With Bradley now under contract with Chess, "the label said, 'Jan can't do any more of your songs unless you're willing to give us publishing rights,' and he refused. That's what changed things for me, because his material was perfect for me. I loved working with him. He was a very kind person, very easy to work with, and I would have been able to do as many songs as Curtis would give me." But as a result of Chess's ultimatum, Bradley and Mayfield never worked together again.

For a long time after that, Bradley's releases just didn't catch on. "I was very sad and disillusioned when I could no longer record Curtis's material. Other writers tried to come up with songs for me, and they just didn't work out too well." Her next three singles did nothing, and Bradley says, "It was only when I decided that I would write a song for myself that I felt good about what I was doing again. I wrote 'I'm Over You,' and that gave me the momentum that I needed to keep going for a while. If you didn't have a record out there that people heard, they'd soon forget about you." "I'm Over You" went to #24 on the R&B charts and #93 on the Top 100, and Bradley was on the charts again.

But after that, none of the singles she recorded did anything on the Top 100 charts, and by the end of the 1960s, Bradley was ready to call it quits—and did, in fact. "I had started college right after high school, but my musical career interests just took over. Then later on, after my musical career was at a point where disenchantment was setting in, I decided to finish college." She completed her undergraduate degree and earned her master's, got married and started a family. Today she's a happy, successful woman who doesn't look back.

Apparently that happiness and upbeat attitude have always been something identifiable in Jan Bradley. Mayfield told *Goldmine*'s Bob Pruter, "Sometimes as a singer it's not how well you sing, it's just that innocence or that certain something about an artist that makes the song appealing. Jan had that innocence in her voice." I mentioned this and Bradley said, "I really appreciate that, and that's where I was at that time. I was sincerely seeking to break into this business, and of course, being so young, I didn't know a lot about what was going on out there. I guess that's where that kind of came from—my demeanor at that time." Through it all, Bradley kept her wits about her and persevered, and along the way she recorded a great beach music classic.

MAXINE BROWN

"OH NO NOT MY BABY"
1964, Billboard #24
Wand 162

Maxine Brown is one of those homegrown artists from the Carolinas who went on to make the big time. Despite the fact that she had more than a dozen chart hits, it's her 1964 classic "Oh No Not My Baby" that has secured her a place in the hearts of beach music lovers everywhere.

Born in Kingstree, South Carolina, Maxine Brown began singing at an early age, and in the late 1950s, she sang with several gospel groups before signing her first recording contract with the tiny Nomar label in 1960. Her first release was her original composition "All in My Mind," which raced to #19 on the pop charts, followed by "Funny," which went to #25. ABC-Paramount then picked up her contract, and conventional wisdom was that she seemed poised to make a major breakthrough. After several singles for ABC did nothing—the highest charted at #98—she left the label and signed with the Scepter subsidiary Wand in 1963. Her first single for Wand, 1963's "Ask Me," stalled at #75, while the next, "Coming Back to You," went only to #99. Two more singles followed in 1964, neither of which charted, and at that point it probably looked like Brown was to be an artist forever on the margins, with her biggest chart hits already behind her.

Then good fortune came her way, oddly enough, at the expense of another group, the Shirelles. By 1964, the Shirelles had charted twenty times in the Top 100 and had had two #1 songs and seven in the Top Ten. One of those #1s, 1961's "Will You Still Love Me Tomorrow," had been written by Carole

King and Gerry Goffin, and they had written another song called "Oh No Not My Baby." The Shirelles recorded the song, but apparently they had decided to alternate lead vocals on the tune, and as a result the management at Scepter felt the recording was a mess. Brown told David Freeland that "they were arguing among themselves about who should be the leader [of the group], so they all took part in this particular song…it sounded like everybody wanted to do their own thing…because they were so far off in taking their own lead, no one knew anymore where the real melody" was. Brown said she was given the song and told to "find the original melody in the song, and you have to do the best you can do with it."

Brown took the song home, put her speakers in her window, turned it on and went out to sit on her front porch. She listened to the song, trying to find the hook, the real melody beneath the Shirelles' dysfunctional recording. She says she thought, "Oh, my God, how am I am gonna get through this?" when she had help from an unexpected quarter: some neighborhood children. "The kids were skipping rope, and after a while the kids kept singing 'Oh no, not my ba-by'…in time with the skipping of the rope." Brown said it hit her then that "'I know a hook when I hear it. Time to go to work!' I left the porch, and I went back in the house and I found a melody in no time…I knew we had a hit."

Brown's instincts were correct. "Oh No Not My Baby" stayed on the charts for seven weeks and went to #24 not only on the strength of Brown's voice but also on a piano intro by Carole King and backing vocals by Dee Dee Warwick. Oddly enough, these layers were added over the same musical tracks that the Shirelles had recorded—their vocals were simply removed. "Scepter did a lot of that in those days," Brown told Freeland. "It saves money from going back to pay the musicians."

Unfortunately, though Brown would have several more charting singles, none would break the Top 40, and 1969's "We'll Cry Together" was her last song to make the pop charts at #73. Eventually she moved into stage work and worked the club scene, and by the 1990s, she was inducted into the R&B Hall of Fame. These days, she also plays in England frequently as the beneficiary of a big following on the Northern Soul scene.

"Oh No Not My Baby" has often been recorded since Brown's original charter; Merry Clayton earned a Grammy nomination for her rendition in 1972, Rod Stewart's 1973 version charted and the song has also been recorded by Cher, Linda Ronstadt and others. Nevertheless, it's Maxine Brown's original version that stands above the others as a beach music classic.

CANNONBALL

"You Keep Telling Me Yes"
1973, did not chart
Blast 101

We were the house band at a club in Myrtle Beach called Dr. Generosity's, which later became the Castaways," Cannonball member Paul Craver told me. "The club was a block south of the Pavilion and upstairs over an arcade. It was a pretty hot club and brought in a lot of national acts." Cannonball wasn't one of those national acts though, and in the early 1970s, they were just like any number of regional bands trying to make it. As the house band, they were fortunate enough to play with national acts that would come to the club and dispense their own special brand of music, while Cannonball labored in the background waiting for their own shot at the big time. That shot would almost come in 1973 with the release of their beach classic "You Keep Telling Me Yes."

In 1973, Cannonball consisted of leader Joe Klinard, Chris Miller, Jack Atchison, Jerry Hutchison, Bucky Cherry, Paul Craver and Phil Garrett. Joe, Bucky and Jerry had written a song for the band called "You Keep Telling Me Yes," and the group had lined up a recording session at Arthur Smith Studios in Charlotte. "The night before we recorded the song," Craver said, "we had played up in Wilmington with the Charlie Daniels Band, who had just come out with this novelty song called 'Uneasy Rider.' After the gig we drove to Charlotte to the studio, where we slept on the floor to record the song the next morning."

Despite their lack of sleep, the group wasn't about to pass up a chance to work with producer Duke Hall, who had also produced the Platters' hits

"With This Ring," "Washed Ashore" and "I Love You 1,000 Times." With Chris Miller on the lead vocals, "You Keep Telling Me Yes" was recorded and became a big success regionally, selling thousands of copies at the beach, where "it became #1 on the beach charts." Unfortunately, as is the case with many regional hits, that sound didn't sell quite as well nationally, so the success of the group's big moment was confined principally to the Carolinas.

Despite the record's solid sound, the group soon disbanded, having recorded just the one record. Craver kept it going for a while until "Bill Griffin of the Castaways Nightclub in Greensboro approached me to put back together the O'Kaysions," Craver said. Though they originally recorded as the New O'Kaysions, for legal reasons they changed the name to the Kays, a name no doubt familiar to many beach music fans. Craver found considerable fame in several other groups such as Shagtime, the Kruze Band and the Men of Distinction, and he has also received a number of accolades for his solo work. But to many beach music fans, he and the rest of Cannonball will always be known for that one record that secured a place in beach music history in 1973. As Craver said, "'You Keep Telling Me Yes' never made it big, but it was a great classic."

THE CATALINAS

"You Haven't the Right"
1967, did not chart
Scepter 12188

"Summertime's Calling Me"
1975, did not chart
Sugarbush 114

W e rehearsed and put 'Summertime's Calling Me' together and recorded it in Charlotte at Reflection Studios," Catalinas founder Gary Barker told me. "We were really excited about it and started performing it everywhere we went, but nothing happened and nobody seemed interested. Finally, we even kinda quit playing it." Looking back, it's surprising that arguably the most important beach music song ever to come out of the Carolinas was a flop at first, a song that has since become the Catalinas'—and perhaps beach music's—signature song. This overshadows the fact that another song they did, 1967's "You Haven't the Right," may be just as good, or better, and though neither was a national hit, the two Catalinas tracks are among the best songs ever to come out of the Carolinas.

The Catalinas are not only one of the longest-lived groups represented in this work, but they have also been one of the most frequently changing. Perhaps that's to be expected of a group first formed in 1958 and still going strong today. In 1967, when they recorded "You Haven't the Right," the group's members were Tom Black, Jack Stallings, Sidney Smith, Johnny Edwards, Tom Plyler, Tommy Garner, Rob Thorne and Johnny and Gary

The Catalinas in the 1960s. *Courtesy of Gary Barker.*

Barker. Gary Barker told me, "'You Haven't the Right' was written by Tom Plyler in 1966…The Four Seasons were really hot back in those days and we had a lead singer, Tom Black, who sang a lot like Frankie Valli, so we—kinda unintentionally—patterned the arrangement after the Four Seasons." The group had the opportunity to record the song, so "we went to Nashville and recorded it in the old Bradley Studio and it was released on the Scepter label." Scepter was home to a number of well-known national recording acts, such as Dionne Warwick, the Shirelles and up-and-comers such as Ronnie Milsap and B.J. Thomas, so it was a big-time label. Consequently, the single did get some airplay. Although the song did well in some regional markets, especially in the South, it didn't sell nationally. The group recorded some other tracks for the label, but none was ever released, so the group carried on, its lineup ever changing, still waiting for that hit that eluded them. And while it might not have been a hit nationally, just a few years later they would record and release that hit, "Summertime's Calling Me," the song that would change beach music forever.

By the early 1970s, the Catalinas' makeup had changed from the "You Haven't the Right" days, and in 1972 Bo Shronce had become the group's lead. There were other personnel changes as well, though Johnny Barker was still the group's keyboardist. His brother Gary told me, "Johnny wrote 'Summertime's Calling Me' when we were going to Boone, North Carolina, to play a job up there. Johnny rode by himself, and when he got the words in his head he wrote them down on a matchbook cover—it was the only thing he could find in his car to write on." As Barker noted, the song initially didn't do anything, and knowing what we know about the popularity of "Summertime's Calling Me" now, it's hard to imagine one of beach music's definitive songs was so underappreciated that after a while it wasn't even on its own group's playlist. "Then in 1980, it hit," Barker told me. "It was all over the radio, so we started playing it again and still play it on every job we play today." Before long it was a jukebox staple up and down the coast. It is still, to most people, the song that epitomizes what beach music is all about.

Indeed, "Summertime's Calling Me" was also probably the record that changed beach music irreversibly. Many artists looked at the regional popularity of the record and started to write songs like it as a result, so "Summertime's" started a new trend: the composition and marketing of songs about the beach designed to be beach music—even if that's not exactly what the Catalinas had in mind when they recorded it. Within a couple of years, bands all over the South were recording songs about beach music itself, about sitting on the beach, about summertime and any and all associated areas of beach music, and as such this song marks the end of the "classic age" of beach music. As a result, claims on the Catalinas' website that say "the song's popularity was the main catalyst that kicked off the modern day beach music renaissance" are true without a doubt. It's for certain that after the regional success of "Summertime's Calling Me," beach music would never be the same again.

The Catalinas in the 1970s. *Courtesy of Gary Barker.*

THE CHAIRMEN OF THE BOARD

"GIVE ME JUST A LITTLE MORE TIME"
1970, Billboard #3
Invictus 9074

"(YOU'VE GOT ME) DANGLING ON A STRING"
1970, Billboard #38
Invictus 9078

"EVERYTHING'S TUESDAY"
1970, Billboard #38
Invictus 9079

By 1968, General Norman Johnson's first group, the Showmen, had split up. But Johnson was far from finished and hardly ready to retire. Instead, he was about to see his greatest fame yet, both as a songwriter and as the distinctive lead voice of the Chairmen of the Board.

At about the same time that Johnson left the Showmen, the famed songwriting team of Holland-Dozier-Holland decided to leave Motown and form the Invictus label, and one of the first acts they signed was the newly formed Chairmen of the Board. Though the original idea was that the group would share lead vocal duties, very quickly it became apparent that Johnson's voice was the most unique, and his vocal on "Give Me Just a Little More Time" confirmed that. The song, with instrumental backing by the famous Funk Brothers of Motown, went all the way to #3 on the pop charts and #2 in England. The record sold more than one million copies, and the group was awarded a gold record by the Recording Industry Association of America (RIAA).

For the Chairmen, the hits would keep on coming. "You've Got Me Dangling on a String" would go to #38 and #5 in England, "Everything's Tuesday" would also go to #38 on the U.S. pop charts and #12 in the UK and the group's first 1971 release, "Pay to the Piper," would go to #13 and #34 on the UK charts. In just two years, with their first four singles, the group had become a powerful musical force.

But Johnson had more going on than just his singing; he was recognized as a major songwriting talent as well. One of his most significant accomplishments was writing "Patches," which Clarence Carter recorded in 1970 and which won Johnson a Grammy award and contributed to his distinction of being named BMI songwriter of the year. He also wrote "Bring the Boys Home" for Freda Payne, the million seller "Somebody's Been Sleeping" for 100 Proof Aged in Soul, the #1 million seller "Want Ads" for Honey Cone and many others.

The Chairmen continued to record, but after "Pay to the Piper" few of their singles charted. Johnson was also having differences with Invictus, because after having so much success as a writer and artist, he felt like he deserved more money, and Invictus did not agree. Johnson eventually left to pursue a solo career at Arista, but because there he didn't feel he had enough artistic control, he left and headed back to the Carolinas in 1978.

Once back home, he re-formed the Chairmen of the Board with original member Danny Woods and new addition Ken Knox. Johnson later said, "For the first time in eight years, I enjoyed performing music without the depression of the music business. I found an independent music industry that was still free of monopoly, politics and categorization." In 1979, Johnson and Mike Branch formed Surfside records in an effort to revitalize a beach music industry they felt was "too dependent on old recordings." They felt

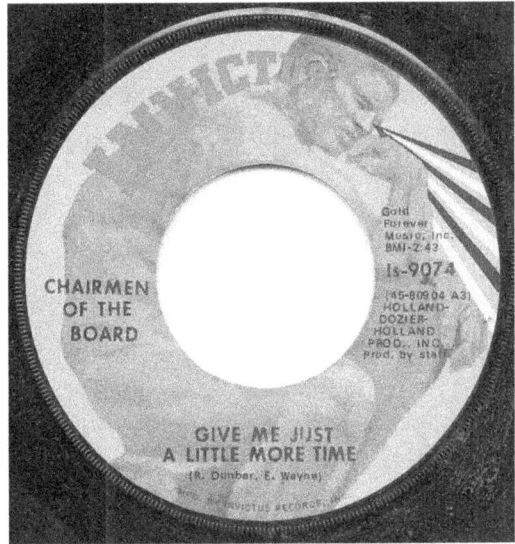

that the genre couldn't survive forever based on just classic recordings of the type celebrated in this book. In that sense, the Chairmen did their part—and then some. Their first release on Surfside was 1980s "On the Beach," followed by "Carolina Girls," "Beach Fever" and many other songs now considered new-era beach music hits.

As a result, the Chairmen of the Board were able to record several classic beach music tunes pre-1975, as well as in the new wave of beach music that came later. Yet for all the accolades and national success, Johnson seemed to prefer the comfortable career as a beach music artist to any other and later even turned down a chance to sign with Motown so he could stay in the Carolinas.

In an obituary article in the *Charlotte Observer* on October 15, 2010, Chris Beachley said of General Johnson, "He told me at times the difference between beach music and a national hit is that a national hit will be out there five or six weeks and gone…He said you write a [beach music hit] and it's there forever. He was the king of Carolina beach music." It is a fitting way to remember General Johnson and the Chairmen of the Board as a whole.

BRUCE CHANNEL

"HEY! BABY"
1962, Billboard #1
Smash 1731

After all these years, 'Hey! Baby' still has legs," Bruce Channel told the author. "It's been included in the soundtracks of numerous feature films, and even now my original recording of 'Hey! Baby' is featured in the long-running musical version of *Dirty Dancing* now playing in London. It really has endured." Channel's "Hey! Baby" certainly has endured and is in fact so well known that not only is it considered a beach music standard but, unlike many songs on this list, it's well known by people who know nothing about beach music. Some beach music lovers may be surprised to know that it was a #1 record and was one of the most popular records not only in the United States, but in the world. Consequently, it lives on as a beach music classic and a seminal rock-and-roll hit as well.

Bruce Channel got the music bug early, playing local dances and clubs back home in Texas in the 1950s. He also played the *Louisiana Hayride* radio show, which featured performers such as Elvis Presley, Hank Williams, Johnny Cash and others. As he wrote and performed his own songs, it soon became not a question of if he'd hit it big, but when. One of those early compositions came about in 1959 "when I wrote 'Hey! Baby' with a friend of mine named Margaret Cobb," he said. He had been playing it in clubs for a while, and over the years the song changed to the point where when he had a chance to record it for Fort Worth producer Bill Smith's Le Cam label in 1961, it had an almost R&B feel to it. The song—which featured

Bruce Channel.
*Courtesy of Bruce
Channel.*

Delbert McClinton's notable harmonica—soon took off, so Smash picked it up for national distribution, and as they say, the rest is history. It shot to #1 on the Billboard charts by March 1962 and stayed at #1 for three weeks, and it also went to #2 in the UK. The song sold over one million copies and was awarded a gold record, and Bruce Channel and "Hey! Baby" were international sensations.

"That began a career of touring with names like Fats Domino, Brook Benton and Curtis Mayfield and the Impressions," Channel told me. "While touring England with Delbert McClinton, we did some shows with the Beatles in their early days when Pete Best was their drummer." Indeed, Channel was the headliner for that show, and a young John Lennon was a fan of Channel's and was fascinated by McClinton's harmonica playing and how Channel had incorporated it into "Hey! Baby." Reportedly, this was what led to Lennon's harmonica use on "Love Me Do," which would go to #1 for the Beatles in 1964 and would encourage the instrument's

Bruce Channel.
*Courtesy of Bruce
Channel.*

use on many other early Beatles songs, such as "I Should Have Known Better," "Thank You Girl," "I'll Get You" and others. As many have pointed out, Channel's "Hey! Baby" therefore had a major formative effect on rock-and-roll.

Over the next few years Channel continued to have records chart, such as "Number One Man," "Come on Baby" and "Going Back to Louisiana." He never had another big chart hit that could match "Hey! Baby," however, and by the late '60s Channel was tired of touring and decided to call it quits as a performer.

Today, Channel works as an active songwriter and publisher in Nashville who has written award-winning songs for John Conlee, Janie Fricke and T.G. Sheppard. But he'll always be identified with "Hey! Baby," the song that was not only a #1 hit and is a beach music staple but inspired the Beatles as well.

TONY CLARKE

"THE ENTERTAINER"
1964, Billboard #31
Chess 1924

Born Ralph Thomas Williams in New York City, Tony Clarke was raised in Detroit. Though early on Clarke was in training to be a chef, he apparently felt the music industry offered a more promising future. His first recording was as Tall Tonio with a backing group called the Mello-Dee's, who recorded "Hod—Rod—Car" for Stepp in 1960. The first single under his own name, "Cry," was recorded on the Fascination label in 1962. Both records failed to find an audience.

Where Clarke was making some inroads, however, was as a songwriter, and two of his songs charted for Etta James in 1963: the classic "Pushover" (#25) and "Two Sides to Every Story" (#63). His success as a writer encouraged Clarke that he did have a future in the music business, so again he tried his hand as a performer. Two more singles on Chess in 1964 failed to chart, but then "The Entertainer" went big. The emotive single, with its organ-played introduction from "I Got Plenty O' Nothing" by way of George Gershwin's *Porgy and Bess*, went up to #31 on the Billboard Top 100 and went into the Top 10 on the R&B charts. The backup singers for "The Entertainer" were another Chess group, the Radiants, who that same year would have a hit with "Voice Your Choice" as well as "Ain't No Big Thing." "The Entertainer" was backed with "This Heart of Mine," a good song that could have been a single release in its own right.

Clarke had three more non-charting singles on Chess, and subsequent singles on other labels in 1967 and 1968 failed to chart as well. However, like many underappreciated '60s soul artists, Clarke found an eager listening audience in England, and while 1967's "Landslide" had fared as poorly as all of his other post-"Entertainer" singles had in this country, it was a huge Northern Soul hit in England, coming in at #15 of Kev Roberts's list of the Top 500 greatest Northern Soul hits of all time. His single "(They Call Me) A Wrong Man" is also a highly regarded Northern Soul disc.

Tragically, Clarke was killed by his wife in a domestic dispute in 1970, before his fame on the Northern Soul scene would have reenergized his career. Nevertheless, beach music lovers will enjoy "The Entertainer" into perpetuity.

THE CLOVERS

"ONE MINT JULEP"
1952, pre-Billboard
Atlantic 963

"NIP SIP"
1955, pre-Billboard
Atlantic 1073

Despite the fact that the Clovers were a successful, seminal, rock-and-roll/rhythm and blues group, they are often overlooked. One would have a hard time believing this if beach music purists are consulted, however. In their circles, "One Mint Julep" and "Nip Sip" are considered two of the most important songs in the oeuvre.

The Clovers got their start in Washington, D.C., right after World War II as the Four Clovers and recorded their first single, "Yes Sir, That's My Baby," for Rainbow records in 1950. The record didn't do much, but Atlantic Records was encouraged enough by what they heard that they signed the group to a contract in 1951. Atlantic's faith was rewarded when the group's first record, "Don't You Know I Love You," went to #1 on the pre-Billboard R&B charts, as did their next release, "Fool, Fool, Fool." Their third Atlantic release was 1952's "One Mint Julep."

Recorded with Buddy Bailey singing lead, its release in March 1952 followed Stick McGhee's "Drinkin Wine Spo-dee-o-dee" by a few years but was the first of a somewhat sustained series of "drinking songs" that would hit the airwaves in the early '50s. The Clovers' record was a departure from the romantic flavored doo-wop that was predominant during the 1950s, and as the story of a man who ended up married all because of "One Mint Julep," it's a humorous take on the evils of drink. The man and a girl he meets have a few "nips," but then he kisses her and one thing leads to another. Later the man tells us, "I got six extra children from a-getting frisky," and so the dangers of drink are all too apparent.

As a humorous cautionary tale, "One Mint Julep" was a hit. While it didn't reach #1 as had its predecessors by the group, it did go to #2. Amazingly, its flip side, "Middle of the Night," also charted, going to #3. In 1961, Ray Charles would also chart with "One Mint Julep" when it went to #8 and #1 on the R&B charts.

Based on the success of these records, the group was at that time considered one of the biggest in the music business, and by April 1953 they had topped two million in record sales. Though a few of their records didn't live up to potential, they were still a solid, successful act and one of the best-known R&B acts in the business because their music was crossing over and becoming popular with white audiences as well as black.

Their next few releases (including 1954's "Your Cash Ain't Nothing but Trash," another beach music favorite) did only moderately well before "Nip Sip" was released in August 1955. "Nip Sip," backed with another fine song, "If I Could Be Loved By You," reached #10 on the R&B charts, but it was one of the last drinking songs to perform well on the charts. This drinking song is toned down a bit, referring to "mellow malts" and "root beer," but the lines "when I wanna get my whistle wet" and "dollar for my nippin and a dime for my lunch" certainly lead one to think more of drinking alcohol than soft drinks.

The group would continue to record into the early 1960s, but musical tastes were quickly changing, and the Clovers' sound was becoming outdated. The Leiber and Stoller–penned semi-novelty song "Love Potion # 9" would make some noise on the charts, probably because it sounded like the material they were writing for the Coasters. It would be their highest-charting pop record and their best-selling single, as well as going to #23 on the pop charts. But like the Coasters, the Clovers would see that the story-song market was drying up quickly, and in fact, "Love Potion #9" would be their last chart record. They would disband in 1961 and re-form, and by the mid-'60s, the group settled in as an oldies act.

When it was all over, the Clovers had had an astounding twenty-one chart records and a legacy as a seminal rock and R&B group. Beach music lovers are most interested in "One Mint Julep" and "Nip Sip," however, records that have been playing on jukeboxes for decades now.

THE COASTERS

"ZING! WENT THE STRINGS OF MY HEART"
1958, did not chart
Atco 6116

Z ing! Went the Strings of Heart" had been recorded a number of times by different artists even before the Coasters did it in 1958. But oddly enough, the Coasters' version wasn't the featured song on the single release, that being instead the #1 hit "Yakety Yak" that was the A-side of the record. Beach music lovers, however, have found something appealing about the throwaway flip side, and so it's this little-known record that did not chart that has come to be regarded as a beach music classic.

The group came about in 1955 when members Carl Gardner and Bobby Nunn of the Robins were reportedly convinced by producers Jerry Lieber and Mike Stoller to start their own group. Billy Guy and Leon Hughes, themselves also veteran performers previously with other groups, were added to the mix to form the Coasters, and the group was signed to Atlantic's then new Atco label. They first charted with "Down in Mexico," which went to #8 on the R&B charts, followed by "One Kiss Led to Another," which charted at #73 on the Billboard Hot 100. It was their next release, "Young Blood," that kicked off a long string of chart hits, going to #8 in 1957, while its flip side, "Searchin,'" did even better by charting at #3.

Soon the group decided to head to New York, but because Nunn and Hughes opted to stay in California the group added new members Will "Dub" Jones and Cornell Gunter. Their first effort was "Yakety Yak," which was a solid #1 smash in 1958. While "Yakety Yak" was wowing crowds, some listeners flipped the 45 over and found an excellent version of "Zing! Went the Strings of My Heart." The song had been written by songwriter James Hanley in 1935, and Judy Garland's 1939 recording was probably the most famous version, though notable artists such as Frank Sinatra and Dinah Shore had recorded it as well. The real anomaly concerning the record, though, is that it is so unlike the Coasters' hits up to that point. The three songs the group charted with in 1957, the year before "Zing!" was released, were "Young Blood," "Searchin'" and "Idol with the Golden Head," and clearly what audiences expected from the Coasters were the novelty or storytelling hits for which they were famous. This may explain why a quality recording such as "Zing!," with Jones and Gunter sharing lead vocals, went unnoticed by many listeners at the time, in that perhaps this love song with a doo-wop feel was so atypical for Coasters listeners that it just didn't register. Producers Leiber and Stoller reportedly considered it the greatest doo-wop song ever recorded, but even Coasters member Carl Gardner didn't think a lot of the song, telling the author only that the song's appeal was due mainly to the bass singing of "Will (Dub) Jones, who was one of the best."

After "Yakety Yak" and "Zing!," the group scored again with "Charlie Brown" (#2), "Along Came Jones" (#9) and many more chart hits over the next few years. Yet the novelty songs that had made them successful were by the early '60s somewhat passé, and so after 1961 they only charted twice more. There was nothing wrong with the quality of the music, but with the British invasion, the Vietnam War and psychedelic rock, by the late 1960s the world had changed, and the Coasters were seen as a link to a simpler, and perhaps by then irrelevant, past.

Like many groups whose histories are detailed in this book, there have been various incarnations of the Coasters since "Zing!" was recorded. "Zing!" itself has been often recorded as well, most notably by the Trammps, whose version hit #64 in 1972. Yet beach music devotees will tell you that whether it's the Trammps, Judy Garland or Ol' Blue Eyes himself singing "Zing! Went the Strings of My Heart," the Coasters, if not first, at least did it best.

THE C.O.D.S

"MICHAEL, THE LOVER"
1965, Billboard #41
Kellmac 1003

For a raucous, party-time beat it would be hard to surpass the Swingin' Medallions' "Double Shot," but the C.O.D.s' "Michael, the Lover" runs a pretty close second. This homage to the sure-to-be narcissistic Michael just failed to make the Billboard Top 40 in 1965, but since "Michael" was the group's debut single, no doubt they continued to expect that their really big hit was just around the corner. The group was a Chicago trio consisting of Larry Brownlee, Robert Lewis and Carl Washington, and in an interview with the *Chicago Defender* they said that after "deciding to form our group and sing...we were turned down by several companies as having no talent." Finally they signed with Kellmac and were told to bring the label a recordable song. Brownlee came up with "Michael" because there was "this guy in our neighborhood who [told] everybody he [was] Michael, the lover. We wrote it, practiced it, got it up tight and then recorded it." "Michael" was the group's very first record, and for that special "female" sound in the background they enlisted the help of Ruby Andrews, who herself recorded "Please Tell Me" for Kellmac in 1965 and would record a number of sides from about 1967 on. When "Michael" shot to #41 on the charts, the future no doubt looked bright indeed.

Unfortunately, "Michael" was to be the high-water mark for the group. All subsequent singles they recorded for Kellmac in 1965 and 1966 stiffed, and by 1967, the group was no more. But as the driving force behind the group, Larry Brownlee wasn't done in the music business. He joined Lost Generation, which had a number of recordings for Brunswick between 1970 and 1974, and then Mystique, which recorded for Curtom in 1977. Sadly, Brownlee died in 1978 without ever scoring that one elusive hit for himself or his group.

Despite its relatively poor showing on the record charts at the time of its release, "Michael" was re-recorded by the Mad Lads. A reported recording by the Jackson 5 is actually a different tune, "Some Girls Want Me for Their Lover," whose name was changed to "Michael the Lover"—no doubt to capitalize on Michael Jackson's first name. Even Kellmac released another version of "Michael" when jazz saxophonist Paul Bascomb recorded it and it was shipped on Kellmac 1004 immediately following the C.O.D.s' recording—and apparently using the same backing tracks laid down by the C.O.D.s. Yet no matter who recorded it or how often it was realized, the first release charted the best, though its moment very quickly passed…until it found a home as a beach music staple.

CORNELIUS BROTHERS AND SISTER ROSE

"TOO LATE TO TURN BACK NOW"
1972, Billboard #2
United Artists 50910

By the time Cornelius Brothers and Sister Rose hit it big in the early 1970s, their sound was already a bit anachronistic; much of their output consisted of love ballads such as Smokey Robinson and the Miracles had built their reputations upon in the 1960s. But while those soft sounds and romantic leanings meant that the group's popularity was not very enduring in the 1970s, it's that very element that has made their songs, especially 1972's "Too Late to Turn Back Now," Carolina beach music favorites.

The core of the group consisted of Eddie and Carter Cornelius of Dania Beach, Florida. Their sister Rose was already in a gospel group and had performed in Las Vegas and on television and joined her brothers at the urging of their mother in 1970. Eddie wrote most of the songs, and by 1971, they had landed a recording contract and recorded their first hit for United Artists, "Treat Her Like a Lady." With its funky, upbeat sound, the record connected with listeners and went to #3 on the Billboard charts, was a million-seller and earned a gold record.

With such significant initial success, the group added another sister, Billie Jo, who was on board for their next single release, 1972's "Too Late to Turn Back Now." The song went a spot higher on the Billboard charts, to #2, and also sold one million copies and earned a gold record. But subtly, the song was different and more indicative of the songs that would come rather than of the formula that "Treat Her Like a Lady" had followed. Instead of a funky, fast beat, "Too Late" featured lush orchestration and anguished lyrics describing the pitfalls of unrequited love and loving too much and too soon. However, it's this sound that makes it a beach music classic and a perfect shag tune as well.

Subsequent singles would follow this same formula, and so the upbeat "Treat Her Like a Lady" was not simply followed by the more melancholy "Too Late to Turn Back Now" but then also "Don't Ever Be Lonely" (#23) and "Never Gonna Be Alone Anymore" (#37). As a result, the group came to be pegged as romantic balladeers, which apparently wore thin with listeners, as each single charted lower than the release before it. After the four charting singles from the first album, by the time their second album was released, 1973's *Big Time Lover*, audiences seemed to have lost interest, despite the fact that the cut "Big Time Lover" may actually be one of their finest tunes. It failed to chart at all.

While the group did have one more Top 100 single—1973's "Let Me Down Easy" went to #96—listeners had abandoned the group by the mid-1970s, and they split up in 1976. Nevertheless, for a moment in time, Cornelius Brothers and Sister Rose was one of the biggest romantic soul acts on the planet, and "Too Late to Turn Back Now" continues to resonate with listeners as a Carolina beach music classic even today.

CLIFFORD CURRY

"She Shot a Hole in My Soul" backed with (b/w)
"We're Gonna Hate Ourselves in the Morning"
1967, Billboard #95
Elf 90002

I was just an R&B singer doing R&B songs, and had no idea what beach music was, what the shag was, nothing. But Rob Galbraith at WNOX in Knoxville kept playing 'She Shot a Hole in My Soul,' and because you could pick it up at night as far away as Myrtle Beach, people at the beach heard the song. That's what got me into beach music. I hope I've made a contribution."

Arguably, Clifford Curry has probably made more of a contribution than most, and his songs on the double-sided hit "She Shot a Hole in My Soul" backed with "We're Gonna Hate Ourselves in the Morning" have gone on to become two of the most popular beach music songs in the genre.

"I got my start singing with local bands in Knoxville," Clifford Curry told the author. "I started with a doo wop group, the Five Pennies, and we got a recording contract with Savoy records. I wrote the first song we did, a song called 'Mr. Moon.' It was a mediocre hit, and it would have done better with better distribution, but it got us on tour with Nappy Brown, a big artist with Savoy at the time." Though the group cut another single, Curry decided to leave the group and head back home. There he joined another group, but Curry wasn't happy as just one of the guys in band, and "about 1959 I decided to become a single artist."

He recorded a few singles for Excello but then decided to join yet another band—but this time as the featured singer. "I joined the Bubba Suggs band

Clifford Curry.
Courtesy of Clifford Curry.

as the featured vocalist. It was the best band I ever played for, and we backed up Solomon Burke and Wilson Pickett, and traveled with Joe Tex and Little Willie John," Curry says. But the wear and tear of the road had become a grind by 1963, and "I decided to go back to Knoxville and got with a local band there and we started playing at a club. I was writing songs and doing my shows, playing every fraternity and sorority party I could."

At the same time he was doing some local recording through Galbraith, who "was a disc jockey at WNOX, the local station. We didn't have a recording studio in Knoxville, but he was on the radio every night from 8:00 to 12:00 and so we'd go out there after 12:00 and record our songs on tape." The amateur recordings and local touring paid off though, because on one trip to Nashville he met producer Buzz Cason. "He'd been out on the West Coast. He was trying to get something started in Nashville, and he liked my voice, and so Buzz called Rob one night and told him,

Clifford Curry. *Courtesy of Clifford Curry.*

'We're going to send Clifford a couple of songs to record.'" As it turned out, "those songs were 'She Shot a Hole in My Soul' and 'We're Gonna Hate Ourselves in the Morning.'"

First Curry and his band recorded "She Shot a Hole in my Soul." "We all felt really good about that record," he says. "Everybody in the studio had a feeling about it, and we believed it was going to chart." Their intuitions were correct, and after being released on Elf records, the song reached #95 on the Hot 100 and #45 on the R&B charts. The flip side of the record was a tune Arthur Alexander had co-written, "We're Gonna Hate Ourselves in the Morning," and though at the time it didn't do much it has become a well-known song too. "Arthur and I were good friends, and we'd hang around and talk about music. He was a great singer and writer, and I was really lucky to get that one." But initially, Cason and even Curry thought the B side was just a throwaway. "We didn't have any idea it was going to be a hit. We had the horn arrangements written out for the horn players to play, and Buzz decided not to use them. He figured it was just a B side so he sent the horn players home." And though the side didn't chart nationally, in the Carolinas it was big, and airplay there got both songs noticed. "I had no idea the songs were going to fit into the beach music thing like they did. I was just a singer trying to have a hit."

Suddenly, Curry was in demand in the Carolinas. "Robert Hunicutt had a club in North Carolina called Williams Lake. He called Rob on the air and said, 'Rob, I'd like to book Clifford over here.' That was my first gig, and Robert was the one who got me to the Carolinas. I played that week, and he had a friend in Myrtle Beach named Cecil Corbett who had the Beach Club. He hired me the next weekend, Easter weekend, when the kids were out on school break. Those two weeks were the best two weeks I ever had in my career. That's what got me into beach music."

Curry would go on to have a long and successful career and would record a number of further singles, though none would have the impact of that first double-sided hit. In the '80s, he had a couple of hits especially tailored to the beach music market, including the fine "Shag with Me." He continues to play the Carolinas and says he's proud that there his songs "are still as popular today as they were back then. People still request the songs today and crowd the floor when I sing them. They get a good response. I'm still writing and performing and singing. So far, I've really been blessed."

BILL DEAL
& THE RHONDELS

"May I"
1969, Billboard #39
Heritage 803

"I've Been Hurt"
1969, Billboard #35
Heritage 812

"What Kind of Fool"
1969, Billboard #23
Heritage 817

We played down in the Carolinas every summer, and during the summer of 1968 people kept requesting 'May I,'" Bill Deal & the Rhondels lead singer Ammon Tharp told me. "Deal didn't like the song at all, and he didn't like the version, and so we changed it up by him putting in a polka-type back beat, like a double time keyboard on it. We did it live on stage, and they went crazy down there. We were there the rest of the week, and we'd get requests to do it two or three times a night. We came back home to Virginia Beach and said, 'Wow—we really gotta record this damn thing.'" Record it they did, and their cover of the Zodiacs' "May I" was followed by two more nationally charting cover tunes that same year. In 1969, when other regional beach music groups appeared to be fading and it was starting to look like the sound might go by the wayside, Bill Deal & the Rhondels carried the torch.

Bill Deal and the
Rhondels. *Courtesy
of Ammon Tharp.*

Deal and Tharp formed the group in 1960 and were happy playing the club circuit in the Carolinas and Virginia, performing old R&B and soul songs. As the '60s progressed, audiences in the Carolinas were clamoring for "beach music," however, and though the Virginians didn't quite yet know what that was—"We played on the beach, but we never knew what beach music was or shagging or that kind of thing," Tharp said—since the same audiences were often requesting the old Zodiacs tune "May I" as an example of beach music, they made the connection. But after coming up with their uptempo version of "May I" to silence the crowds' requests, they suddenly realized that "it was really working the way we were doing it." Faced with the song's obvious popularity, they decided to press some copies. "Bill was the one responsible for putting that whole thing together musically. Then he told me how to sing it," Tharp said. "My voice was unique, but not a good voice. I understand that, but he knew what I could do, and he was the only one who could figure out, 'You can go this high, or you can go this low. This is what you need to do and how you need to do it.' He was involved with the vocals, the instrumentation, everything. He loved recording, and that's good because I wasn't really that fond of recording in the first place." Deal apparently had a gift for it, because "May I" did well when pressed and came to the attention of Heritage Records.

The group landed a recording contract, and the single took off. "May I" entered the Hot 100, and then the Top 40, before it stalled at #39.

"Then we did 'I've Been Hurt'—I don't really know why we chose it next, but Deal just had an insight on how to do those songs in our style," Tharp said. "We were doing Tams songs in our set and liked the songs, but thought, 'Let's change it up for a national audience.'" Their remake of the Tams' 1965 single would do a little better than its predecessor, stalling at #35—and would even be voted song of the year in Mexico. Next they'd release a remake of another song in their act, the 1964 Tams' hit "What Kind of Fool," and it would surpass both previous releases, going all the way to #23. In just one year, with their updated versions of the Carolina beach music sound, the group had become a solid national act.

But with success came constant touring, and the time in the spotlight was taking its toll. "We were going to New York every week promoting and doing TV and radio, and traveling and playing," and when they played Madison Square Garden with Neil Young, Deep Purple and Crazy Elephant, "we realized, 'We're in the wrong place here.' We're a bunch of short-haired, Ivy League–looking guys doing Motown and having to play with these rock bands, and we weren't into the rock thing, which was coming on really strong. Every time we played up there we'd go against a rock band, and while they loved our records, they'd come on and blow our ass away with their rock-and-roll." So as the touring got old, and since "we were making decent money, but we weren't getting rich, we thought, 'You know, we could do this at home and just play the Southeast.' We were kind of homebodies—we loved Virginia Beach—and we figured financially we could do just as well and not be gone all the time. So we said bye-bye. We thought success was fine—but 'nah.'"

The group took it home, and though they still played the clubs and toured, by removing themselves from the national spotlight and focusing on more regional venues, they were able to maintain some semblance of normality in their lives. It served them well, and they were popular for many years in the Carolinas and Virginia, always playing to packed houses. Though Bill Deal has passed away, Ammon Tharp continues to perform those great standards that brought the Carolinas' beach music sound into the national spotlight in 1969. "I don't get tired of it, and if I don't do those three songs every night, I'm upsetting people. But I don't mind doing those songs at all—I'm still having fun forty years later." And while the world and the music have changed since then, the sound of Bill Deal & the Rhondels has remained timeless and takes listeners back to those carefree days in the late 1960s—summer nights, crowded clubs and warm draft beer. And beach music is all the better for it.

ERNIE K. DOE

"MOTHER-IN-LAW"
1961, Billboard #1
Minit 623

"TE-TA-TE-TA-TA"
1961, Billboard #53
Minit 627

K. Doe had a pretty big ego," Deacon John Moore said. "K. Doe always thought he was the best there was in show business and called himself the 'Emperor of the Universe.' The only performers he felt were up to his standards were James Brown and Sammy Davis Jr!" Moore, who played backup on "Mother-in-Law" and "Te-Ta-Te-Ta-Ta," as well as many other hits from the New Orleans music scene, also recalled that Ernie K. Doe often said, "At the end of the world, there's only gonna be two records playing—'The Star Spangled Banner' and 'Mother-in-Law.' He was quite a character." Though Ernie K. Doe had just one big chart hit, there was a lot more to the man and his music than that solitary hit record. "Despite his braggadocios nature," Moore told me, "he was a really good showman on stage. Everybody can attest to that."

Born Ernest Kador Jr. in New Orleans, like many soul artists his first experience singing was in the church, but as he got older he became more interested in a future as a performer of rhythm and blues. Eventually he had the opportunity to record a few solo sides for various labels before he finally ended up in 1959 at Minit, where he had the chance to work for the now-legendary Allen Toussaint. His first single didn't do anything, though the next, 1960's "Hello Lover," generated enough regional interest that it reportedly sold 100,000 copies. His next release was the 1961 smash "Mother-in-Law."

"Mother-in-Law," written by Toussaint, was a playful tune in the vein of many of the Coasters hits. K. Doe later claimed (though Toussaint disputed it) that he found the song in a trashcan after Toussaint had thrown it away and decided that he wanted to perform it. K. Doe told the *Chicago Tribune*'s Dave Hoekstra that the song resonated with him because "my mother-in-law was staying in my house. I was married 19 years, and it was 19 years of pure sorrow. When I sang 'Satan should be her name,' I meant that."

One thing that really made the song work was the contribution of backup Benny Spellman, who at the time was also a struggling artist for Minit. Spellman agreed to help out on "Mother-in-Law," and his bass voice can be heard echoing K. Doe by singing the words "mother-in-law" throughout the record. Between K. Doe's playful lyrics and Spellman's resonating bass, the song hit #1 on both the pop and R&B charts.

But the song's success also caused a rift between Spellman and K. Doe. "Well, K. Doe went out on a national tour when 'Mother-in-Law' was hot, and Benny was a little peeved at K. Doe because K. Doe didn't take him out on the road with him. Benny was upset because, he said, "'Mother-In-Law'" wouldn't have sold if they didn't have my bass voice in there'—that's really what Benny thought sold the record," Moore remembers. "There was a little disagreement between them."

But the little disagreement became a big disagreement—and led to blows. "K. Doe had just come back off his successful road tour, and they went back to the studio to do a follow up to 'Mother-in-Law' with the same kind of line called 'Get Out of My House,'" Moore said. "Benny was there, and K. Doe and Benny were in the booth for the singers and you could just see the tension between the two of them. All of a sudden, K. Doe and Benny came tumbling out of the booth with their hands at each other's throats. They were rolling on the ground, fighting, and Allen Toussaint called off the session!" Moore laughingly told me. "We assumed they were arguing about who made the record sell, over whether or not it was Benny's bass voice. Later on, I also heard it might have been over a woman!"

Though "Mother-in-Law" had made K. Doe a star, his next song, 1961's "Te-Ta-Te-Ta-Ta" wasn't a big hit—although over time it has come to be regarded as a beach music classic in its own right. "That was written because Ernie had his trademark style of singing where he'd go 'ah-ah-ah,'" Moore said, "and so Allen wrote 'Te-Ta-Te-Ta-Ta' to rhyme with that." Recorded at that same follow-up session with "Get Out of My House," "Te-Ta-Te-Ta-Ta" would go to #53 on the Top 100 and #21 on the R&B charts. K. Doe had a few more low-charting records before 1962's "Popeye Joe" (#99) was his last chart record.

By 1964, K. Doe had left Minit, and perhaps his biggest success story post–"Mother-in-Law" came when he released "'Here Come the Girls" in 1970. It failed to find an audience, but in 2007, a British pharmacy chain used the song in a commercial and K. Doe's version was re-released and went to #43 on the British charts. In 2008, the British girl group Sugarbabes released a cover version of the song called "Girls," which went to #3 in England, and nearly four decades after its initial release, K. Doe's music was in the Top 10 again.

Ernie K. Doe never lived to see the resurgence of his popularity through "Here Come the Girls," however. After a career in radio in the 1980s, K. Doe opened the Mother-in-Law Lounge in New Orleans in 1994. He frequently performed there, often in a cape and a crown in his "Emperor of the Universe" persona. A flamboyant performer until the end, he died from liver and kidney failure in 2001. But despite the fact that he had only one really big hit as far as the general public was concerned, the recordings of "Mother-in-Law" and "Te-Ta-Te-Ta-Ta" are more than enough to endear him to beach music fans forever.

THE DRIFTERS

"Up on the Roof"
1962, Billboard #5
Atlantic 2162

"Under the Boardwalk"
1964, Billboard #4
Atlantic 2237

"I've Got Sand in My Shoes"
1964, Billboard #33
Atlantic 2253

"Kissin' in the Back Row of the Movies"
1974, did not chart
Bell 45600

Over the course of nearly fifty years, the Drifters sold more than 200 million singles and 100 million albums. But for all their success, the Drifters had one of the most disjointed histories of any group in music. And while personnel turnover meant the lead vocals were handled by as many as fifteen different singers, they still managed to produce some of the greatest beach music ever recorded, including "Up on the Roof," "Under the Boardwalk," "I've Got Sand in My Shoes" and "Kissin' in the Back Row of the Movies."

Clyde McPhatter left the Dominoes in 1953 to form his own group, the Drifters. With McPhatter singing lead, they'd have the #1 R&B hit, "Money Honey," in 1953, but McPhatter was soon drafted and sold his controlling share of the group to manager George Treadwell. Johnny Moore joined the group—now consisting of Gerhart Thrasher, Andrew Thrasher, Bill Pinkney and Jimmy Oliver—and took over as lead singer. Their first recording with Moore as lead, "Adorable," went to #1 on the R&B charts and was followed by classic tunes such as "Ruby Baby" and "Drip Drop." However, there was tension between the group and their manager, and after Pinkney asked for more money he was fired, and Thrasher quit as well. Soon Moore and Hughes received their draft notices, and the Drifters, it seemed, were done.

But Treadwell had heard a young singer named Benjamin Nelson (later to become Ben E. King) and hired him and three members of his group, the Five Crowns (Charlie Thomas, Doc Green and Elsbeary Hobbs), to become the Drifters. Their first song was "There Goes My Baby," which went to #2 on the charts and had the distinction of being the first rock record to incorporate strings.

While the earlier Drifters' music had more of a doo-wop feel, the new Drifters music, which included "This Magic Moment" (#16), "I Count the Tears" (#17) and "Save the Last Dance for Me" (#1), had a more elegant sound, and the #1 hit seemed to confirm that they'd found the right formula. But despite the group's success, King felt that he should be making more money, and predictably Treadwell disagreed. King left, and once again the Drifters had to recruit a new lead singer. This time it was Rudy Lewis. "Some Kind of Wonderful"(#32), "Please Stay"(#14) and "On Broadway"(#9) followed, as well as the beach music classic "Up on the Roof."

"Up on the Roof" was written by two of the '60s' greatest songwriters, Carole King and Gerry Goffin. The song isn't about the beach, and in fact climbing "way up to the top of the stairs" to relax on the roof of an urban building seems to be the antithesis of what beach music is all about. Nevertheless, it may be the idea of getting away from one's troubles that appeals to beach music lovers, and listeners in 1962 found that appealing as well. The song went to #5 on the Top 100 and #4 on the R&B charts and has been one of the most popular and everlasting of the group's hits; in 2004, the song was included in *Rolling Stone*'s 500 Greatest Songs of All Time, and it appears on the Rock and Roll Hall of Fame's list of the "500 Songs that Shaped Rock and Roll."

Lewis's voice had carried "Up on the Roof" perfectly and no doubt would have done as well with the classics "Under the Boardwalk" and "I've

Got Sand in My Shoes." But Lewis didn't sing those two hits, because the night before "Under the Boardwalk" was supposed to be recorded he died unexpectedly. Though the cause of his death was never determined, those close to Lewis claimed he was a binge eater and may have choked to death in his sleep.

Fortunately, Johnny Moore had returned to the group in 1963 and had actually sung lead on "I'll Take You Home" (#25). He took over the lead on "Under the Boardwalk" and recorded a classic that would go to #4 on the charts. The song was written by Arthur Resnick (who would later write "Good Lovin'" for the Rascals and "Yummy, Yummy, Yummy" for the Ohio Express) and Kenny Young (who would write "Arizona" for Mark Lindsay) and was reportedly a bit faster and more upbeat originally than in the recorded version. But given the group's despondency that day, it ended up having a slower, more melancholy sound. There's something very deeply heartfelt about the song that has struck a chord with listeners for decades.

Having had their highest chart record in four years, the group wasn't about to alter the formula and next released "I've Got Sand in My Shoes," another Resnick and Young gem and one very similar in style and sound to "Boardwalk." Beach music lovers see this not as too much of a good thing but as another example of a great song about the beach, the feel of sand and warm days and being with the one you love. "Sand" didn't chart as high as "Boardwalk," going only to #33, but other than their next release, "Saturday Night at the Movies," which peaked at #18, it was the last Top 40 hit the group would ever have in America.

By the late '60s in the United States, the Drifters were no longer a hot property, so they headed to England, where they were still big. Signing with Bell Records, their fourth release, "Kissin' in the Back Row of the Movies," went all the way to #2, and the Drifters were officially back—in England, at least. Though the record only reached #83 on the R&B charts in the States (their last chart record of any kind in the United States), copies could be found on jukeboxes throughout the Carolinas. The group would go on to have six Top 10 hits in England, including 1976's "You're More Than a Number (In My Little Red Book)," before Moore left the group in 1978.

Since then there have been several different touring groups with the Drifters' name, but whoever was singing those songs then or now, the group is perhaps the biggest and most successful of all the beach acts, having recorded numerous hits the world over. To beach music lovers, though, their worldwide popularity is not the main selling point—for us, their music is simply the essence of what beach music should be.

THE EMBERS

"FAR AWAY PLACES"
1969, did not chart
MGM 14167

W hen we started out, we did mainly rhythm and blues, but because we played functions for older people too we also performed old standards like 'Begin the Beguine' and things like that," Embers founder Bobby Tomlinson told the author. "Far Away Places" was also one of those old standards, but the version they played in the late '50s would evolve into more than just a run-of-the-mill throwaway standard, and through what was almost an accident, it would become the group's biggest hit of the classic beach music era.

When teenagers Bobby Tomlinson, Jackie Gore and Blair Ellis started the original Embers back in the '50s, like most regional bands they played fraternity parties and any other type of gig they could get. Their focus was mainly on rhythm and blues and soul, the type of music that would become known as beach music just a few short years later. After several years on the club circuit, they opened their own club in Raleigh in 1965 and then another in Atlantic Beach in 1968, and in their clubs they played with acts such as Jackie Wilson, Jerry Butler and the Drifters. They opened for the Beach Boys in 1966 and the Rolling Stones in 1968 and recorded several albums. As a result, they were not only popular, with a successful performing career, but they were successful businessmen and club owners as well.

It was at that Atlantic Beach club one night that something happened almost by accident. "In 1968, Archie Bell had 'Tighten Up' out with that 'dut duh duh duh duh duh' rhythm and beat to it," Tomlinson said. "One night

The Embers in the 1960s. *Courtesy of Bobby and John Tomlinson.*

we were performing—there were probably 1,500 to 2,000 kids in there—and we were playing 'Tighten Up.' We got into a grove, just jammin', and Jackie then led right into and started singing 'Far Away Places,' and it went over. And it worked so well that we started doing it all the time." As one of those old standards, "Far Away Places" had been written in 1948 and recorded by the likes of Bing Crosby, Perry Como and Dinah Shore. Clearly it was a well-known song at one time, but by setting that old standard to that "Tighten Up" beat, the Embers—now consisting of John Thompson, Durwood Martin, Johnny Hopkins, Ray Rivera, Bobby Tomlinson and Jackie Gore—made it their own and were soon playing it for audiences throughout the area.

And people started to notice. "Agents and promoters would come into the area to promote their records," Tomlinson said. "A lot of them used to come by the Embers Club and hang out. A friend with ABC booking out of New York heard us do 'Far Away Places,' and he was friends with Bob Crewe, who had done 'Music to Watch Girls By' and who was with MGM records. We made a tape, sent it to him and he signed us to a contract. They did the music out there with professional musicians, and then they flew two producers out and the vocals were recorded here."

The Embers in the 1970s.
Courtesy of Bobby and John Tomlinson.

"They released it and it was doing great, and we thought we were on the way," Tomlinson said. "It was being played everywhere, and we heard it was played in Vietnam all the time. Then Bob Crewe was fired from MGM, and every act he'd just signed went out with him. They pulled the plug on us." Consequently, the record stopped getting pushed nationally and never quite became the hit many thought it had the potential to be. Still, the group continued to perform, and though outside of the parameters of this book, arguably their biggest musical moment came in 1979 when they recorded "I Love Beach Music," one of those seminal modern beach music tunes that changed the genre forever.

Over the years, the Embers have become one of the biggest regional groups that never made it big nationally yet helped define the genre. They still play throughout the year, and Tomlinson says, "Audiences still like to hear 'Far Away Places,' and it's probably still the song we're identified with. Maybe not more so than 'I Love Beach Music,' but 'Far Away Places' is definitely our song—even these kids today know it." Remarkably, the Embers are still at it just as strong as ever, and "Far Away Places" remains a true classic and thrills audiences to this day.

THE FANTASTICS

"SOMETHING OLD, SOMETHING NEW"
1971, Billboard #102
Bell 977

For most of their long recording career, they were known as the Velours. As a well-known doo-wop group, the Velours still have a substantial following in those circles, and in fact, it was as a doo-wop group of more than a decade's duration that their reputation was established. But for a short while they worked as the Fantastics, and it was during this period that they scored their one monster beach hit, "Something Old, Something New."

The group started out in the 1950s as the Troubadours, and by the time they changed their name to the Velours in 1956 the lineup consisted of Jerome Ramos, John Cheatdom, Donald Heywood, Kenneth Walker and Marvin Holland. After playing the Apollo Theater in October 1956, they recorded "Can I Come Over Tonight," which would be their first chart record. The song—which Ramos had written for his girlfriend—was released in June 1957 and would go to #83 on the charts. Two recordings later, "Remember" would also chart, and as two of their three recordings had charted in less than a year, the future certainly looked promising for the group.

But for whatever reason, the group had already reached its high-water mark. Over the course of the next ten years, they would jump from label to label, but none of their records charted, and members came and left the group periodically. In 1968, the group—now consisting of Ramos, Cheatdom, Heywood and Richard Pitts—decided to change their name to the Fantastics, perhaps deciding that the Velours name was too closely tied to the doo-wop tradition, a musical phase that had long since passed, not to mention that they hadn't really had any notable success with the name in more than a decade.

After the name change, they recorded five singles between 1969 and 1971, and it was in '71 that they were handed the Roger Cook song "Something Old, Something New." Cook was the writer responsible for hits such as "Here Comes that Rainy Day Feeling Again" by the Fortunes, "I'd Like to Teach the World to Sing" by the New Seekers and "Long Cool Woman in a Black Dress" by the Hollies, so in the early 1970s, he was riding a tremendous wave of success. The Fantastics recorded Cook's "Something Old, Something New" for the Bell label in 1971, and though it is a fine tune, obviously well written and exceptionally well sung by the former Velours, it struggled up the charts, bubbling under at #102 in the United States. In the UK, however— one is almost tempted to say "as usual," concerning the British ability to spot potential beach music hits better than Americans—it went all the way to #9. Two releases later, they had their only charting record in the United States, 1971's "(Love Me) Love the Life I Lead," which went to #86.

Within a year, the group's lineup changed yet again, and after two more singles their recording career as the Fantastics was over. The old Velours name was even resurrected later, so in truth the group existed as the Fantastics for only a short time in their long and storied career. Nevertheless, in the minds of beach music lovers, that brief moment as the Fantastics led to the indisputable beach classic for which the group is held in great esteem today.

THE FOUNDATIONS

"BABY, NOW THAT I'VE FOUND YOU"
1967, Billboard #11
Uni 55038

"BUILD ME UP BUTTERCUP"
1969, Billboard #3
Uni 55101

"Those recordings have brought me a whole lot of happiness over the years," Foundations lead singer Clem Curtis told the author. That happiness was well deserved, because the Foundations recorded some of the biggest hits of the late 1960s. Right out of the gate they hit it big with their first single, "Baby, Now that I've Found You," and with their follow-ups the groundwork was in place for what should have been a long and productive career as front-rank recording artists. Yet almost as soon as their first single charted, the group's dynamics started to change, and within three years the Foundations had completely disintegrated.

Considering that the majority of the most popular 1960s British groups had an edgier sound, the Foundations were surprisingly soul-based. The group's multinational and racial makeup also contributed to their uniqueness, and in addition to Trinidadian lead singer Clem Curtis, there were two Jamaicans, a Dominican and a mix of Brits. In 1967, this diverse group came to the attention of producer and songwriter Tony Macaulay, and although he had not yet become the hot property he would be in the 1970s after writing hits such as the 5th Dimension's "(Last Night) I Didn't Get to Sleep at All," David

Soul's "Don't Give Up on Us Baby," Edison Lighthouse's "Love Grows (Where My Rosemary Goes)" and others, he was on his way. According to John Kutner and Spencer Leigh in *1000 UK #1 Hits*, when Macaulay originally heard the Foundations, he thought they were terrible, but because he had a hangover he believed it was more his head than his ears that didn't like their sound, so he agreed to write for the group.

"At first there were two songs offered to us," Curtis told me. "One was 'Let the Heartaches Begin,' but instead we chose 'Baby, Now that I've Found You' because I didn't think I could sing 'Let the Heartaches Begin' as well. 'Baby, Now that I've Found You' just seemed to be a much better song for me." It was a good choice, and though initial sales were sluggish, eventually the record took off, benefiting from the English soul boom and interest in the Motown sound. Consequently, "Baby" raced to #11 in the United States and #1 on the UK charts, although Curtis admits, "I really had no idea it would be such a success." (Interestingly enough, the song the group refused, "Let the Heartaches Begin," would also hit #1 in England for Long John Baldry.)

As the first British band with a major soul hit, the Foundations were big, and their follow-up single, "Back on My Feet Again," hit #18 in the UK. But things weren't going well within the group. Despite the success of their first single, Macaulay admittedly didn't like the group's sound any better now that he *didn't* have a hangover, and he was trying to push their output in a more pop-oriented direction. In the meantime, Curtis says he was feeling the need to go out on his own, and "Sammy Davis Jr. had recommended that I come to the United States" because Davis felt that Curtis would be a draw there and he had the potential to be a huge solo act. "So, I was about to leave the group," Curtis told me, just as Macaulay told them he'd co-written another song he wanted them to record. Even though it wasn't enough to make Curtis stay, even as he left he sensed the song might be another big one. "It's true I had nothing to do with the song at the time, and then I realized I really liked it," he said. That song was "Build Me Up, Buttercup."

It's rare that a group can survive the departure of a lead singer, but the Foundations managed with new singer Colin Young singing lead on "Buttercup." It's a catchy, joyful-sounding tune, even though the lyrics are actually about a man who has been jilted repeatedly by the girl who is the love of his life. Despite the fact that he "can't take anymore," and she is "untrue," he's attracted to her "all the more." Please, he says, "don't break my heart." Listeners adored it, and "Buttercup" went to #2 in the UK and to #3 in the U.S. in 1969, and the Foundations were back on top once again.

Their next single was another great Macaulay-penned song, "In the Bad, Bad Old Days," which was a UK Top 10 hit but only went to #51 in the U.S.

Macaulay parted ways with the group, and with the Foundations recording songs by other writers the magic was gone. Since then though, "Baby, Now that I've Found You" and "Build Me Up, Buttercup" have become classics. Curtis says, "'Baby, Now that I've Found You' is still a crowd pleaser, a song that is fun to do," and one he still performs "because everyone in my age group and young people like hearing it too." "Over the past forty-three years I have sung these songs all over the world," and he agrees that "Buttercup," especially, is pretty much universally recognized. Indeed, because commercials, movies and television shows have used the song, it's known by millions. Both songs have been embraced in the Carolinas and are now considered beach music classics.

THE FOUR TOPS

"BABY I NEED YOUR LOVING"
1964, Billboard #11
Motown 1062

"I CAN'T HELP MYSELF"
1965, Billboard #1
Motown 1076

"I JUST CAN'T GET YOU OUT OF MY MIND"
1974, Billboard #62
Dunhill 4377

A combination of factors makes any entry on the Four Tops and their music among the most difficult in this book. Like the Drifters and the Tams, many of their songs could have made this list, and narrowing it down to just two or three left out some great music. Like the Temptations, they are a product of the Motown music machine and one of the best-known musical groups to come out of the 1960s, yet they still had considerable success beyond that decade. With these advantages—and the fact that their songs are some of the most singable and danceable of the Carolina beach music classics—they perhaps stand at the top of the list of the many great artists whose music has been covered in this book.

Levi Stubbs, "Duke" Fakir, "Obie" Benson and Larry Payton started singing together in high school in 1954 as the Four Aims. Payton's cousin Roquel Davis sent a demo tape to Chess Records, and the label signed them and changed their name to the Four Tops. Nothing they did at Chess or at several other smaller labels after that met with any success, but in 1964 they signed with Berry Gordy at Motown, and with the dynamic Holland-Dozier-Holland team writing for them, their first hit was "Baby I Need Your Loving," which went to #11 in 1964. The song, which would go on to sell more than one million records, was popular not only for the Four Tops but would also go on to be a hit for others, including Johnny Rivers. It was the Tops' version that was first and best, however, prompting *Rolling Stone* magazine to rank it as one of the "500 Greatest Songs of All Time." They followed this with "Without the One You Love" and "Ask the Lonely" before they released their first really big hit, "I Can't Help Myself."

With the Funk Brothers laying down the instrumentation, the Holland-Dozier-Holland-penned song featured Stubbs's agonized voice singing—some have likened it to shouting—"Sugar pie, honey bunch/I'm weaker than a man should be." Indeed, many call the song "Sugar Pie Honey Bunch" rather than its real title. But whatever you call it, the group had finally found its sound. In an interview with Pete Lewis for *Blues and Soul Magazine*, Stubbs said, "'I Can't Help Myself'…I mean, we musta sung that song so many times I wake up in the NIGHT singing it! In a way it's our theme song!" That "theme song" went to #1 on the pop charts and the R&B charts, was the group's first single to chart in England and made *Rolling Stone*'s "Greatest Songs" list as well.

"I Can't Help Myself" was followed by an astonishing twenty-five more chart hits while at Motown, including such Top 10 hits as "It's the Same Old Song" (#5), "Reach Out and I'll Be There" (#1) and "Bernadette" (#4). But Holland-Dozier-Holland left Motown in 1967, and Stubbs told Lewis, "We were hurt, shattered, and a bit confused. We still got hits, but suddenly we weren't getting all those songs custom-written for us." Then when Motown tried to lowball its bid for the group's new contract in 1972, they left for ABC-Dunhill.

Right away, it was apparent that Motown had unwisely let the group go too soon. Their first release for ABC, "Keeper of the Castle," went to #10 in 1972, and in 1973 they followed up with hits such as "Ain't No Woman" (#4) and "Are You Man Enough" (#15). The year 1974 brought a song that, though not a national success, is one of the best-loved beach tunes of all—"I Just Can't Get You Out of My Mind." Like "I Can't Help Myself," it is often known in beach music circles by another name, "Call Me," which alludes to the fact that the song begins "Call me, were the last words I remember…" (Indeed, at a performance in the late 1970s in Myrtle Beach, at first the group seemed a bit perplexed as the audience kept shouting that they wanted to hear "Call Me" until they finally figured out what the audience was requesting.) While many other Tops songs are beach classics, perhaps it's "Call Me" that seems most distinctly to be a beach song, maybe because like many other beach music cuts it isn't all that popular with anybody outside of the Carolinas anymore. It wasn't a big hit for the group; not only did it score low on the pop charts (#62), but it only made #18 on the R&B charts and it didn't chart at all in England. But beach music fans love it.

The group would go on to have a number of other hits, including another beach favorite, "When She Was My Girl," in 1981. And unlike many other groups that constantly changed over the years, only death could split up the group, which never varied its lineup once in forty-four years. Though Stubbs, Benson and Payton have all now passed away, Fakir continues to perform with a new group and sing those great classics.

THE PROPHETS/GEORGIA PROPHETS

"I Got the Fever"
1968, did not chart
Smash 2161

"California"
1970, did not chart
Capricorn 8006

Roy Smith called me and said, 'You gotta come over to my house right now—I just wrote your next hit record," Billy Scott told the author. "I said, 'Oh, really?' and he said 'Yeah, I just hope you're gonna like it.' So I drove over to his house, and I sat down beside him at the piano. He started playing, and the hooks in that song just threw me back—'I love you, I love you, I love you yes I do.' I went, 'Oh man!' I mean, you know, it got me right then. Then he started playing the verses. It went back and forth like that and I thought, 'Oh my God, this is going to be a great tune.'" And "I Got the Fever" was, and is, a great tune, and with another of their songs, "California," the Georgia Prophets have two of the greatest Carolina beach music classics of all time.

Billy Scott had been a singer before serving in the army, and after he was discharged, Billy and his wife, Barbara, worked singing backup vocals in the Augusta area. While in the studio in June 1965, Augusta musician Tommy Witcher happened in and heard them singing and asked the two to join his band, the Scottsmen, which consisted of Witcher, Freddie Williamson, Walter Stanley and Jimmy Campbell. Soon the group changed their name

The original Prophets. *Courtesy of Billy Scott.*

to the Prophets, and like many regional groups at the time, they played gigs whenever and wherever they could get them. They cut their first record, "Talk Don't Bother Me," for Delphi in 1966, and based on airplay in the Carolinas, Jubilee picked up the single. Though it didn't make any noise nationally, when their next single, 1967's "Don't You Think It's Time," came out on Delphi and was getting regional play, Jubilee picked up that single too, though with yet again the same results.

The group continued to play throughout Georgia and the Carolinas, and in 1968 they landed a record deal with Smash just in time for the release of "I Got the Fever." Scott notes that Roy Smith wrote not only "I Got the Fever" but also "Don't You Think It's Time," "For the First Time" and "Nobody Loves Me Like You Do." But as soon as Smith played "Fever," Scott was convinced it would be a hit. "Roy was really excited about the song too, and then we called Tommy. He came over, Roy played it and Tommy said, 'That *is* a great song.' So we drove to Atlanta and recorded it, and the rest is history." As the band recorded it, Scott had a feeling it would be big too. "One reason was because the band was young, and it was the early era of beach music, anything that we recorded back then probably would have been a hit if it really had a good hook." Though the song didn't make the national charts, it did sell well in certain areas of the country, especially in the South. Scott thinks that one reason the song has been so successful as a beach classic was that recordings then often had a different, more soulful feel. "Back then the band played all at one time, and recording was electrifying. It wasn't where you'd have a bass player come in and play later on. Everybody would play at the same time, and what a groove they got. Today you go in there and the band records some, and then if the bass player screws up you go back and lay it down later on. It's nowhere near as exciting as it was back in 1968."

Suddenly the group was bigger than ever, and that forced a change. "We changed our name to the Georgia Prophets in 1969 for several reasons. There was a group called the Prophets in Florida that threatened to sue us, and there were also several other groups named the Prophets, and it was confusing for fans. There was also *another* group in Virginia named the Prophets. We'd be booked somewhere and people would call and be told the Prophets were playing, and they'd ask, 'Which Prophets?' Told it was us, people would say, 'Oh, you mean the Georgia Prophets.' So our fans really changed our name for us," Scott says.

The group next recorded "For the First Time" on Double Shot records and finally had a record receiving national notice, as it went to #36 on the R&B charts. Things were going well, but even so, "Tommy decided that we needed to add another female vocalist. He decided to hire Janet Helm, and when Janet came to the group, she said, 'I've got this song ya'll might be interested in recording called "California."' I asked, 'What's that got to do with the Carolinas? It's kind off of to the left there, you know—left coast music!' But the group wanted to hear the song, and Janet, who played the acoustic guitar, played it for us and sang, 'California is a callin' me, California is a where I should be, California 90023.' I said, 'What does 90023 mean?' And she explained, 'That's the zip code where I lived.'" Scott says Helm explained that she wrote the song because, "'I moved to California, but didn't stay long, because things just weren't going right. But I just loved it out there and so on my way home I decided to write about it.' So she wrote it and offered it to us, the band rehearsed it and got it all together before we got to the studio, but we didn't work on the background vocals. So Barbara and Janet came up with the background vocals on the way to the studio, and I just sat there listening to them in the car on the way to Atlanta. We got there, put it all together, and recorded it in one take."

So yet another beach music classic was born.

The group would go on to record several other beach classics, including "Nobody Loves Me Like You" (1970) and "I Think I Really Love You" (1971), and today Billy Scott continues to perform and is known to many as the "Ambassador of Beach Music" for his efforts to promote and preserve the genre. "I'm very pleased that you're doing what you're doing," he told me, "because if we don't write about it and sing about it, we could lose it. Beach music is the greatest music in the world," he said. The Georgia Prophets and their hits "I Got the Fever" and "California" are a couple of reasons why beach music is the greatest music in the world.

THE GLOBETROTTERS

"RAINY DAY BELLS"
1970, did not chart
Kirshner 63-5008

W ell, we'd worked on the idea of doing an album for quite some time," Meadowlark Lemon told me. "When we recorded 'Rainy Day Bells' for the album I thought it was a nice, catchy little tune, but that's it. I didn't think it would be as popular as it is or do what it's done. It's amazing to me that it's still so big in the Carolinas." Maybe even more amazing is how that song and album came about, which was as the result of a confluence of several powerful forces that were affecting the direction of pop music in the late '60s and early '70s. There was the rise of made-for-television musical groups, such as the Monkees and the Partridge Family, cartoon musical groups, such as the Archies and Josie and the Pussycats, and bubblegum music, being turned out by studio groups such as the Ohio Express and the 1910 Fruitgum Company. It was from this odd amalgam that "Rainy Day Bells," was born.

When cartoon groups were big in the late '60s and early '70s, someone at Hanna-Barbera suggested that a cartoon based on the Harlem Globetrotters might be a good idea. CBS liked the concept as well, so from 1970 to 1972, twenty-two episodes featured characters based on real Globetrotters "Meadowlark" Lemon, "Curly" Neal, "Geese" Ausbie, "Gip" Gipson, Bobby Joe Mason and Pablo Robertson, along with several fictional counterparts. In the mold of other cartoons at the time, the "gang" would find themselves up against evildoers but would reign supreme in the end, despite some hilarious misadventures.

Also like other cartoons at the time, such as the Archie Show and Josie and the Pussycats, an attempt was made to cash in on the cartoon's popularity by having the characters release an album and a few singles, trying to milk every bit of marketability from the show and targeting the pocketbooks of the parents of those kids watching television on Saturday mornings. Consequently, an album was produced by Jeff Barry and released on Kirshner records in 1970, and one of the songs on the album was released as a single, the Neil Sedaka and Howie Greenfield tune "Rainy Day Bells."

While "Rainy Day Bells" was a good song, it was not a big seller, even though it was rumored that it was the team themselves singing it. That makes for a good story, but it wasn't quite true. "Yes, I sing background on the record," Lemon said. "Not the best background singer, but I did sing background. But they had some great professional studio singers and musicians there to put that thing together, and they, not the team, sang it." Lemon was actually the only team member there, and reportedly among the other singers were vocalists such as Sammy Turner (who had charted with "Lavender Blue" in 1959), J.R. Bailey (formerly of the Cadillacs of "Speedo" fame), Robert Spencer (also of the Cadillacs and Crazy Elephant) and Rudy Clark (singer and also writer of such hits as "The Shoop-Shoop Song"). With that pedigree, the song should have been a hit, but perhaps the combination of the cartoon backdrop and a doo-wop sound that had faded from popularity a decade before relegated the well-crafted tune to obscurity. And as there was no real Globetrotters group to tour to follow up the album, "Rainy Day Bells" was a one-hit wonder for the studio group in every sense of the word. "Rainy Day Bells" was the studio group's only significant contribution.

As for the song, Lemon is still impressed by its longevity. "I think 'Rainy Day Bells' has remained popular because it has an infectious melody," he says. "It's one of those songs that when you hear it, over and over and over, you begin to like it even more. Neil Sedaka did the song before we did, though his version didn't catch on like ours. Now why, I have no idea. But I realize that our version is still a hit up and down the East Coast. People talk to me about it all the time. It's amazing." Maybe it's because it's a tune far superior to many others by groups that have been around for decades. It's a real beach music phenomenon.

THE INTRIGUES

"IN A MOMENT"
1969, Billboard #31
Yew 1001

I n a Moment" by the Intrigues is one of those fast-paced, almost anthemic singles due to its chant-like refrain of "Don't you know that I love you, love you, love you, love you, love you girl, oh I love you so awww…" In fact, it's a song that's short on a variety of lyrics and long on repetition; nevertheless, it's one of the finest beach songs of the 1960s and a precursor of the sophisticated Philadelphia soul sounds that would grow to titanic proportions during the 1970s.

The Intrigues consisted of group members Alfred Brown, James Lee, James Harris and Ronald Hamilton, and their first recordings were small-label platters such as "Soul Brother" for Toot Records and the first recording of "In a Moment" on the small, local Philadelphia label Bullet in early 1969. "In a Moment" was a big song on a small local label, due no doubt to the arranging and production skills of Bobby Martin and Thom Bell (Bell's track record was superb: before the Intrigues, he had produced for the Delfonics and would later do the same for the Stylistics and the Spinners, among others). "In a Moment" was eventually picked up by the larger Yew Records as the second 45 Yew released and rose to #31 on the charts before stalling. At that time, both Yew Records and the Intrigues seemed poised for great things.

But like so many artists and small labels in the annals of music history, both artist and label had already peaked, unbenownst to either of them. "In a Moment" would be the Intrigues' biggest hit, and they would climb no further than the bottom reaches of the Billboard Hot 100 with both "I'm Gonna Love You" in 1970 (#86) and "The Language of Love" in 1971 (#100), despite the fact that the latter was co-produced by the talented Van McCoy. After six singles on Yew and then two on the Janus label, the group disbanded. Though they attempted a comeback in 1985 with the song "Fly Girl," their return effort met with no success on the Billboard Hot 100 chart. Similarly, the Yew label, after producing just thirteen singles, the last of which was the Intrigues' "Mojo Hannah," by 1971 had folded as well.

THE INTRUDERS

"TOGETHER"
1967, Billboard #48
Gamble 205

A long with the O'Jays, no group personifies Philadelphia soul like the Intruders. Known for a string of popular hits in the late '60s and early to mid-1970s, the group was a product of the Kenny Gamble and Leon Huff phenomenon. Yet for all their success in the 1970s, it's their song "Together," a record that didn't even break the Top 40, that most appeals to beach music lovers throughout the South.

The Intruders originated in Philadelphia in the late 1950s and originally consisted of Sam Brown, Eugene Daughtry, Phillip Terry and Robert Edwards. In the early 1960s, they had the opportunity to lay down a few tracks, but recordings such as "I'm Sold On You" (1961) and "This Is My Song" (1962) didn't really do anything. It wasn't until 1965, when they paired up with Gamble and Huff, who had just launched Gamble Records, that their careers took off. Despite the fact that the Intruders had yet to record a hit, Gamble and Huff felt like they were the perfect group to launch their fledgling label, so the very first disc the label released was the Intruders' 1966 single "(We'll Be) United," backed with "Up And Down the Ladder" on Gamble 201. The record peaked at #78, which wasn't bad for a new label's first release.

In fact, four of the first five records the new label released were Intruders efforts. "(We'll Be) United" was followed by two more releases before their fourth single for the label, and their first release of 1967, the beach classic

"Together." Listeners liked the song, and it climbed to #48 on the Hot 100. Though not a big hit, it was followed by the double-sided charter "Baby I'm Lonely" (#70) and the fine "A Love That's Real" (#82), and thus began a long string of first-rate hits for the group. Next up was 1968's "Cowboys to Girls," the Gamble and Huff–penned classic that sold more than one million records, earned an RIAA-certified Gold Record and went all the way to #6 on the pop charts and #1 on the R&B charts. By this time, it was apparent that Gamble and Huff's faith in the group had paid off—though in retrospect that comes as no surprise, considering how intuitive the two were at picking hit acts in the years that followed.

The Intruders would have a string of fourteen chart hits over the next few years, including "(Love Is Like a) Baseball Game" (#26) and another beach favorite, "I'll Always Love My Mama" (#36) in 1973. During this period, Sam Brown would leave the group, Bobby Star would step in as lead singer and then Brown would rejoin the group once again. Along with the O'Jays and Harold Melvin and the Blue Notes, the Intruders would be one of the most visible groups on the Philadelphia music scene in the '70s before disbanding in 1975.

The group eventually re-formed, and today they tour with only two surviving original members. Despite the fact that "Together" wasn't one of their biggest hits, it is the record of theirs that has been covered the most. Both Gladys Knight and the Pips and the Three Degrees recorded the song, but it was the one-off group Tierra that had the biggest hit with it in 1981, taking it to #18 on the pop charts and #9 on the R&B charts. As a shag classic, however, nothing surpasses the original.

THE ISLEY BROTHERS

"THIS OLD HEART OF MINE (IS WEAK FOR YOU)"
1966, Billboard #12
Tamla 54128

Considering that today the Isley Brothers are regarded as a near-legendary soul group, it's surprising that early on they had a hard time staying with a label. Maybe even more surprising is that based on their early chart success with raucous party tunes such as "Shout" and "Twist and Shout," and later for funk recordings such as "It's Your Thing," they are best known by beach music aficionados for the vastly different and soulful "This Old Heart of Mine."

Like many groups, the Isley Brothers had their origins in gospel and then turned to doo-wop in the late 1950s. Rudolph, O'Kelly and Ronald Isley would record discs for four different labels before they landed at RCA, thanks to their being recommended by Jackie Wilson. Their second release for RCA was 1959's "Shout," and while today the song is well known and seen as a seminal rock-and-roller, it only reached #47 on the charts, though eventually it would sell more than one million copies and become their first gold single. Because they weren't able to follow it up with another hit, however, RCA dropped them from the label. They went to Atlantic and then Wand, where they did a cover of the Top Note's "Twist and Shout" in 1962, which charted at #17 and was their first big hit (though the Beatles' cover version went to #2 and is now better known). After a few more records at Wand, they released singles for several different labels before finally landing at Berry Gordy's Motown subsidiary, Tamla, in 1966.

Gordy saw the group's potential, and indeed he gave them a song by the famed Holland-Dozier-Holland songwriting team (with Sylvia Moy) to record called "This Old Heart of Mine (Is Weak for You)." The song had been intended for the Supremes, but at the time they were riding a string of eight #1 hits and didn't really need it. With the Funk Brothers providing back up and Ronald Isley on lead, the single raced up the charts to #12 on the pop charts and #6 on the R&B charts, the Isleys' biggest hit to that point. While that Motown beat is no doubt what has endeared it to beach music lovers, Isley's anguished cry for his girl to return his love would resonate with listeners then and later; Tammi Terrell, Rod Stewart and others would also record the song, and Stewart and Ronald Isley would record a duet in 1989 that would top the adult contemporary charts.

Despite this powerful and very promising start, after "This Old Heart of Mine" they had six more charting releases at Tamla, but "I Guess I'll Always Love You," another beach favorite, was their highest charter in the U.S. at #61. They'd leave Tamla and form their own label, T-Neck, where they went on to their greatest success with records such as the funky "It's Your Thing" (#2), "That Lady" (#36), "Fight the Power" (#4) and others, and their lineup changed too. They disbanded in the 1980s, though they worked together on and off thereafter. Yet despite the fact that they had more than eighty chart records between 1959 and 2006, it is that classic Tamla single, "This Old Heart of Mine," for which they are best remembered by Carolina beach music lovers.

J.J. JACKSON

"BUT IT'S ALRIGHT"
1966, Billboard #22
Calla 119

It's not a prerequisite that a great beach recording be recorded in the South, and in fact most were not. In J.J. Jackson's case, "But It's Alright" wasn't even recorded in this country, but in England, where beach music's cousin Northern Soul reigns supreme. On both sides of the Atlantic it was a great, robust classic.

J.J. Jackson didn't enter the world with his catchy, alliterative name but instead was born as Jerome Louis Jackson, and as such he recorded with a group in the '50s known as the Jackaels. They cut a song called "Oo-Ma-Liddi," which went nowhere. He also worked as an arranger and songwriter, and his songwriting credits from the early '60s include songs such as the Shangrilas' "It's Easier to Cry," the flip side of their hit "Remember (Walkin' in the Sand)." This song still lists him as merely J. Jackson, but when the Pretty Things charted in England with another Jackson creation, "Come See Me (I'm Your Man)," in 1966, he was by that time taking label credit as J.J. Jackson. A big, nearly three-hunred-pound man in the physical mold of Billy Stewart and with a soulful "belter" voice like Otis Redding, his talent as a singer was recognized in the mid-1960s, and he was signed by the Calla label.

His first release for Calla was a big one, a song he wrote with Pierre Tubbs and recorded in England, "But It's Alright." Rock critic Don Waller claimed that with "two notes, then four and then two notes, then four," it had an opening riff "strong enough to levitate a bloc of communists." This rocking 1966 soul number certainly appealed to listeners, rising to #22 on the Billboard charts before stalling. His next Calla recording, "I Dig Girls," only charted at #83, but nevertheless two consecutive records, both charters, seemed to bode well for the singer. His next song, on Calla 133, "Four Walls," didn't chart, and unbeknownst to anyone at the time, Jackson would never have an original issue chart again. "But It's Alright" would chart again, however, when Warner Brothers bought the Calla catalogue and re-released the song in May 1969 and it climbed to #45.

Jackson's chart fame had passed, though he continued to perform in England and cut albums and singles into the early '70s. Perhaps the question most often asked is if this is the same J.J. Jackson who was an MTV VJ in the 1980s. He is not, and in fact as of this writing, the MTV Jackson had passed away, while the "But It's Alright" Jackson was still doing an occasional gig, belting out his special moment in recording history.

JEWELL AND THE RUBIES

"KIDNAPPER"
1963, did not chart
ABC Paramount 10485

D oug and I would get together, we'd sit down and I'd play the chords, he'd plot them and we'd go from there," Jewell and the Rubies keyboardist Hershey Deville told me. "When we came up with 'Kidnapper,' Doug and I were sitting there and he said, 'How does this sound?' He hummed, 'Da-da-da-da-da-dah, da-da da da-da,' I played it on the piano and he started singing the chorus, 'Kidnapper, bring my baby back to me.' We filled in the rest later." So it was from just a simple chorus that, deep in the heart of Cajun country, Jewell "Doug" Douglas, Hershey Deville and the Rubies produced one of beach music's greatest songs. And while the group didn't get the national recognition that many of their fellow Louisianans such as Ernie K. Doe, Brenton Wood and Willie Tee did, nevertheless, their soulful strut "Kidnapper" made it east and became a staple of jukeboxes throughout the Carolinas.

"Jewell Douglas came to James Stephens High School in Ville Platte as the band director—most of us were in the marching band—and when the Rubies started almost all of us were in eighth or ninth grade," Deville said. After Douglas recruited Deville "because he found out I had an ear for music," they formed the rest of group from Douglas's other students or former students and added Sylvester Weatherall, Ralph Frank, Milton Lazar, Rogers Thomas, Lannis Fontenot and Leroy Alfred to make Jewell and the Rubies, though like all bands there would be a few changes over the years. They played local gigs all over Louisiana, but with "Kidnapper," they knew they had something special, "so we went to the [La Lousianne] studio in Lafayette. We spent a couple of weeks, going back and forth, adding, deleting, until we got it right and we liked it. But when we recorded it, we had no idea it would be such a hit."

The song was magic. Some of the intricacies of the song are probably lost on younger listeners today because the song is so era-appropriate, and in fact, it is by far the most '60s referential song on this list. The lyrics mention '60s legal and detective shows such as *Route 66, Perry Mason, Hawaiian Eye, Peter Gunn, The Untouchables* and others. Television references aside, "It just had that beat," Deville says. "After we recorded it everybody wanted us to play it. Out of twenty songs, we'd play 'Kidnapper' for what seemed like two hours. People would say, 'Play that again,' and we would." The song was in such demand in the South that ABC records became interested, and they released it on ABC Paramount 10485. But the song didn't sell nationally, and David Rachou, son of Carol Rachou, owner and founder of La Lousianne Records, said he remembers his father telling him that it was because "not long after that, the Payola scandal broke and ABC had over half of the top ten songs on the chart so they decided to kill the song before it went anywhere." Even though it wasn't a national hit, the group was still in demand. Deville said, "A guy heard us play at a club in Lafayette, and he wanted to sign us up and take us out on the road." For the group to go on tour behind a single on a national label might have positioned them to break into the big time, but it was not to be. "We were all still in school—I was a junior in high school—but my mother said, 'No, you're not quitting high school to go on the road to travel.' All of our parents said the same thing. So there was no national tour."

Deville says that they did write some more songs, but nothing else really clicked with listeners like "Kidnapper" had. Rachou said that though the group "did come back to the studio to try a follow-up recording session, the material wasn't very good, so that was pretty much it."

That was it indeed. The group's inability to travel to support their records, coupled with the failure to record that big follow-up single to "Kidnapper," meant that though the guys played together for a few more years locally, they never got another shot at the big time. "But we were well known in Louisiana," Deville told me, "playing R&B, our songs and everybody else's songs. We were the #1 group in Louisiana for a while." When the guys graduated from high school and started to go off to college, the group just ceased to exist. Jewell Douglas later moved to Chicago, where he passed away some years ago. Still, though the group may be gone, they left us with one of the greatest beach songs of all time.

THE JEWELS

"OPPORTUNITY"
1964, Billboard #64
Dimension 1034

W e met Smokey McCallister in New Jersey, and he took us to New York
and let us hear some songs before we decided on 'Opportunity,'"
Sandra Peoples Bears said when I asked her where they came up with
their big hit. "We recorded some other songs around that time also, but
'Opportunity,' that was the big one." "Opportunity" was indeed big, and in
the Carolinas it has been regarded as a major beach music hit for decades—
and may be as popular on the beach now as it was in '64.

Like many groups in this book, Sandra Peoples Bears, Grace Ruffin,
Margie Clark and Carrie Mingo went through several incarnations before
they emerged as the Jewels. They originally came together in Washington,
D.C., in the late 1950s as the Impalas. Ruffin was the cousin of the then
relatively unknown Billy Stewart, who was a piano player for Bo Diddley's
band, and under Diddley's tutelage the Impalas recorded for Checker in
1961. They changed their name to the Four Jewels in 1962 and recorded for
the Start label and then for Chess again, but none of their recordings made
a dent in the charts. By this time Stewart was emerging as a star in his own
right, and the girls did a stint as backup singers and "sang backup on many
songs with Billy," Bears said, including vocals on "Reap What You Sow," the
A side of "Fat Boy." By this time, Martha Harvin joined the group to replace
Mingo, and the group recorded several more singles, some produced by yet
another of their famous mentors, James Brown.

The Jewels. *Courtesy of Sandra Peoples Bears and Beverly Johnson.*

Despite the fact that Bears noted that "we had some local hits as the Four Jewels," nothing yet had made any noise nationally. It was apparent that many in the record business saw their potential, however, and it finally paid off for Dimension in 1964. "Our manager was Smokey McCallister, who we'd met previously while we were performing at the Howard Theater. He asked about managing us, but we didn't get together until later because we were under contract with someone else at the time." Having changed their names to simply the Jewels (Clark wasn't touring with the group, so appearing as just the Jewels seemed more appropriate), their first record with their new name was "Opportunity." With Sandra Bears's dynamic lead vocal, the record started to pick up steam—but it didn't happen overnight. "Well, when we recorded it, it didn't come right out—it was a few months—and we were hoping it would come out sooner," Bears said. "I thought, personally, it could have been promoted a little more. I think when it started taking off on its own they started to push it more, but I think that had it been promoted more from the beginning it may have done even better." Hearing it today one would have to agree, as it only managed to reach #64 on the pop charts that December, despite its riveting sound.

Their next record, "But I Do," a remake of the Clarence "Frogman" Henry hit, didn't break the top 100, nor did "several songs we recorded around the same time, like 'Smokey Joe'" and some others. Not long afterward, the

The Jewels. *Courtesy of Sandra Peoples Bears and Beverly Johnson.*

Dimension label folded, and then post-"Opportunity" recordings by the group on the Federal and Dynamite labels stalled as well.

"After that, we toured backing up James Brown," Bears said, "and we're on one of his albums of the show with James Crawford, Bobby Byrd and some others." After backing up Brown for a few years they disbanded about 1968. Though the Jewels really never had that big, big moment on the charts, "Opportunity" is nevertheless one of the finest singalong and dancealong songs in the annals of beach music.

ROBERT JOHN

"IF YOU DON'T WANT MY LOVE"
1968, Billboard #49
Columbia 44435

Robert John had an interesting, odd and spotty recording history. He charted with teenage anthems and remakes of others' records and ultimately had a #1 record more than twenty years after his career began. It's not one of his chart toppers, however, but one of his records that didn't get a lot of national playtime that has endeared him to beach music lovers—his 1968 release "If You Don't Want My Love."

In the 1950s, Robert John Pedrick was like many aspiring singers who were enthralled by the doo-wop scene, and he had a voice well suited for harmonious singing. That magnificent voice didn't go unnoticed, and by the time he was just twelve years old, as Bobby Pedrick Jr. he had recorded "White Bucks and Saddle Shoes," which peaked at #78 in 1958. None of his subsequent releases over the next couple of years charted, and he next did a spin as a frontman for the group Bobby and the Consoles, releasing a New York regional hit in 1963 called "My Jelly Bean," which failed to chart nationally as well.

In 1966, after nearly a decade of recording, he decided to try his hand as a record producer and songwriter, and in order to make a clean sweep he even started going by the new name "Robert John." According to Fred Bronson in *The Billboard Book of #1 Hits*, "Eventually he began to write songs with a partner, Mike Gately," and apparently a Columbia Records producer heard John singing on a few demos and decided to give him a try behind the microphone once again. The result was 1968's "If You Don't Want my Love," a record that gave John the opportunity to show off his full vocal range. Penned by Gately and John, the song built to a climax that clearly demonstrated that John's voice was as strong and versatile as contemporaries Frankie Valli and Lou Christie, both of whom had done exceptionally well during the '60s.

The song almost broke the Top 40 by reaching #49, yet rather than build on this first moderately successful single and give John a chance to exhibit how his songwriting skills could take advantage of his vocal abilities, the *If You Don't Want My Love* album that Columbia released to capitalize on the single was a dud. In addition to "If You Don't Want My Love," it contained only seven songs, and six of those were cover tunes. John recorded one other Columbia single, "Don't Ever Leave Me," which "bubbled under" the Top 100 at #108, but he then left Columbia. He went to A&M Records and then Atlantic, and it was there that he had his greatest success up until that point with a cover of the Tokens' "The Lion Sleeps Tonight," despite the fact that he really didn't want to do the song. Although the song (which was produced by original Tokens singer Hank Medress) went to #3, sold more than one million copies and was awarded an RIAA gold record in 1972, John was frustrated. Bronson notes that John told Steve Pond of *Rolling Stone* that Atlantic "didn't have enough faith to let me do an album. I decided that if that's what happens after a [hit] song, then I just wasn't going to sing anymore." After he barely charted with "Hushabye" at #99 (another cover tune) and released the magnificent beach classic "You Don't Need a Gypsy" in 1972, he quit the music business.

In 1978, after John had held an assortment of jobs, including carrying bricks at a New Jersey construction site, producer George Tobin found him and got him recording again. John wrote a song called "Sad Eyes," and after a series of failures to place it, EMI picked it up. After recording for almost twenty-two years, John finally had a #1 chart-topper. John would stay with EMI and would continue to do originals as well as covers of many songs that required a unique sound or a falsetto. He would chart with Eddie Holman's "Hey There Lonely Girl" (#31), and his cover of the Four Seasons' "Sherry" (#70) would make some noise. He would then move to Motown and do another cover, this time of the Newbeats' 1964 #2 hit "Bread and Butter" (#68) in 1983. It would be his last chart record.

Robert John recorded for a lot of labels under several names and recorded more covers of other artists' songs by far than any beach music artist in this book. Yet it's fitting that the record that beach music lovers most appreciate is his self-penned "If You Don't Want My Love"—a true beach music classic.

BOB KUBAN AND THE IN-MEN

"THE CHEATER"
1965, Billboard #12
Musicland 6548

"I look back and I wonder," Bob Kuban said in an interview for this book. "We could have been as big as a lot of bands at the time. We had everything going, we had good writers, we were playing good music, everything was coming together, and then this bastard came along and screwed it all up." Kuban has reason to wonder, as the story behind "The Cheater" is one of the most compelling, and at the same time disturbing, in rock-and-roll and beach music history. First, there's the mystery of how a highly successful band with three straight Top 100 hits in one year could suddenly by the end of that year exist no more. Then there's the story of how, in a twist of fate that could have been foreseen by no one, charismatic lead singer Walter Scott was murdered by the man his wife was allegedly cheating with. In some ways, the group's tortuous history has overshadowed a great song and a beach music classic—as unfortunately happens when life is sometimes stranger than fiction.

Bob Kuban started his first band during his senior year of high school, but it wasn't until he founded Bob Kuban and the In-Men in 1965 that things really started to click. The In-Men featured lead vocalist "Sir" Walter Scott, and they established themselves as a very popular regional group. But at the height of the Vietnam War, just being in a popular band wasn't enough to keep you out of the draft, so in order to qualify for their draft deferment most of the members of the band were also college students. While teaching

Walter Scott and Bob Kuban.
Courtesy of Bob Kuban.

or going to college kept them out of the army, it also meant they couldn't tour for too long or too far away from home, but as a regional act early on that wasn't much of a problem. But once they recorded "The Cheater" everything changed.

"The Cheater" was recorded in St. Louis on the Musicland label, and originally the song was written in the first person ("Look out for me, I'm a Cheater"). "But I wanted to do a song that had excitement to it, had some energy and had a good driving tempo," Kuban told me. "So we added a bridge, and put it in the third person." These alterations made the song a winner, and nationally, the record took off. It peaked at #12 on the Billboard charts and earned a gold record in the process. Bookings across the nation followed, and the group played with the Turtles in San Francisco and with Otis Redding at Whiskey a Go Go and appeared on television on programs such as *Where The Action Is* and *American Bandstand*. Internationally, the song did well too, and it went all the way to #1 in Australia. They were so big in Australia, in fact, that they were scheduled to do a nine-week tour there, and it seemed that with a Top 40 hit and international appeal, the group's ship had finally come in.

Unfortunately, the U.S. government's rules about draft deferment brought their plans to a screeching halt. The group discovered they couldn't go to Australia because if they weren't working as teachers or in school they'd lose their deferment. Kuban says that the draft board told him that if they went, they would immediately be classified 1-A and be drafted, and that effectively put an end to any plans the group had for traveling abroad. So instead of the planned tour, they headed back to the studio and recorded the follow-up to "The Cheater," "The Teaser." But there were problems there as well. Kuban says, "I hated the song, and even today I have never played it live. I fought with our manager about releasing it after 'The Cheater' because I knew a hit record needed a strong follow-up, and 'The Teaser' wasn't it. I just knew that it wasn't a good song." Over Kuban's objections, their manager released the song anyway, and despite its clear inferiority to "The Cheater," "The Teaser" actually climbed to #70 on the charts. Next up that year was a cover of the Beatles' "Drive My Car," which went to #93. No matter how one looked at it, three chart records in a row in one year did seem to promise great things ahead for the band.

But trouble was brewing, and unbeknownst to Kuban, their manager, of all people, was trying to break up the group. "Mel Friedman was the manager at the time, and at first things were going very well with him, but it got so he had an agenda, which unfortunately didn't involve me. He started causing a lot of problems because he saw the advantage of Wally breaking away for his own purposes. Wally was a very good lead singer, and he was like a Fabian or Frankie Avalon, a good showman, a good-looking guy, and Mel obviously wanted to pull Wally away from the band." The next thing Kuban knew, "despite the fact that we had a hit record, all of a sudden, the band was breaking up, and guys were leaving. At the time I was completely blown away, I was in shock really, because I didn't know why this was happening." Lead singer Walter Scott left and opted for a solo career, though neither he nor the other members of the group matched the magic they had held collectively. "It was only years later that Wally told me what had happened, because by then he realized what an opportunity we had and that Friedman had blown it for all of us. He got hold of good talent and screwed it up."

Despite the acrimony of the group's split, nearly twenty years after their dissolution, the band was preparing for a big reunion concert when Walter Scott mysteriously disappeared in December 1983. In time, a bizarre tale unfolded that has even been the subject of its own book. Scott was tied up, shot in the back and thrown into a cistern, where his decomposed body was finally found in 1987. Eventually, the boyfriend (and later husband) of Scott's second wife was found guilty of the murder (and his own wife's) and given two life sentences; Scott's ex-wife was also convicted of hindering the prosecution of the murder and sentenced to five years in prison. It is obviously a cruel irony that saw the lead singer on "The Cheater" meeting his untimely end in the way that he did.

Kuban continues to perform to this day. He has recorded some solo efforts, and he has a band that is highly regarded and plays a variety of venues across the Midwest. One can't blame him for thinking as he does, though, that "if Mel Friedman had stayed out of everything, we probably would have been a very successful group for many years." Fortunately, their moment in the spotlight, even if brief, did produce "The Cheater," a classic that is still a favorite of beach music lovers even today.

BARBARA LEWIS

"HELLO STRANGER" b/w
"THINK A LITTLE SUGAR"
1963, Billboard #3
Atlantic 2184

Trying to decide on just one—or even two—Barbara Lewis songs to qualify for this list is a daunting task. "Baby I'm Yours" (1965), "Make Me Your Baby" (1965) and "I Remember the Feeling" (1966) are all prime candidates and could just as easily be here instead of "Hello Stranger." In fact, the flip side of "Hello Stranger," "Think a Little Sugar," is probably the most viable contender of all of Barbara Lewis's songs even though it was just a B side. What's obvious is that Lewis belted out a lot of classics, and "Hello Stranger" backed with "Think a Little Sugar" packs perhaps the greatest one-two punch of any single on this list.

Barbara Lewis first recorded for the Karen label with "My Heart Went Do Dat Da" in 1962, and though a regional success, it wasn't a chart force nationally. Despite this, she showed potential, and after moving to Atlantic, her first release there was "My Momma Told Me" in 1963. The next single, 1963's "Hello Stranger," would indicate that the potential was reality and much, much more. Lewis's self-penned song was backed by the Dells, and the song was arranged by Riley Hampton, who was at the time also working with the great Etta James. A soulful cut that, oddly enough, only mentions the title once in the song—and that in just the first two words—Lewis's single raced to #3 on the Billboard charts (#1 on the R&B charts), and Barbara Lewis was a star.

Lewis went on to record a number of dynamite singles with Atlantic, such as the Van McCoy–produced "Baby I'm Yours" (1965, #11), "Make Me Your Baby" (1965, #11) and "Make Me Belong to You" (1966, #28). Another great beach music hit that wasn't a Billboard chart hit is 1966's "I Remember the Feeling," a great shag classic. From 1966 through 1968, Lewis recorded five more singles for Atlantic and then three for Enterprise in 1969 and '70 and one for Reprise in 1972. Despite the beauty of her voice, her sophisticated sound apparently didn't connect well with listeners in the late '60s and early '70s, so her moment had passed.

The passing years would see "Hello Stranger" recorded by a number of artists, both major and minor, including the Capitols, Fire and Rain, Darius, the Supremes and Four Tops, Yvonne Elliman, Carrie Lucas, Martha Reeves and the Vandellas and Queen Latifah. None of these has equaled or surpassed the original, however, which, coupled with its flip side "Think a Little Sugar," may be the strongest two-sided beach hit ever recorded.

MARTHA AND THE VANDELLAS

"JIMMY MACK"
1967, Billboard #10
Gordy 7058

Hearing "Jimmy Mack" today, it's hard to believe that though Martha and the Vandellas recorded it in 1964, Motown felt it wasn't suitable for release, shelved it and didn't release it until three years later. But there's a story behind that delayed release, and the holdup didn't affect the song's popularity at all; in fact, "Jimmy Mack" went on to be one of the group's biggest hits.

Martha Reeves moved to Detroit at an early age and formed her first vocal group in 1958. She later joined the Fascinations and then the Del-Phis in 1960. Reeves was by this time also working as a solo act singing in nightclubs, and it was at one such club that Motown's Mickey Stevenson spotted her and told her to come in for an audition. Like several other Motown artists at the time (such as Diana Ross), Reeves worked as a secretary while doing backup vocals when needed, and in fact, Reeves arranged for her former Del-Phi bandmates to record the backup vocals along with her for Marvin Gaye's "Stubborn Kinda Fellow."

Soon Motown offered the group their own recording contract, and now known as Martha and the Vandellas, Reeves, Rosalind Ashford and Annette Sterling had their first chart hit in 1963 with "Come and Get These Memories," which peaked at #29 on the pop charts. This was followed by "Heat Wave" (#4), "Quicksand" (#8), "Dancing in the Street" (#2), "Nowhere to Run" (#8) and other hits up through 1966. Throughout this period, the group's lineup would fluctuate, with Reeves being the one constant. But the group was popular, surpassed only by the Supremes as a girl group Motown draw, and they performed on *The Ed Sullivan Show*, *Shindig*, *Ready Steady Go*, *American Bandstand* and others.

Around the same time "Dancing in the Street" was recorded, the group also recorded "Jimmy Mack," a song written by Motown's famed Holland-Dozier-Holland writing team. The story goes that Lamont Dozier attended a dinner where the late songwriter Ronnie Mack was being honored, and Dozier wrote the song with him in mind. In the song the group pleads for Jimmy Mack to come back, especially since there are now other boys in the picture. It was a good song with a good sound (as its chart status would eventually prove), but nevertheless, Motown decided not to release it. Apparently the powers-that-be at Motown felt that the song might be too controversial if audiences thought the group was pleading for Jimmy to return because it could be interpreted that he was in Vietnam, and that might make people edgy. Consequently, the recording was stuck in the vault, and in 1967, with the condemnation of the Vietnam War more vogue than taboo, the single was finally released. It shot up the charts, peaking at #10 and #1 on the R&B charts. In fact, the song was the last Top 10 song the group would ever have. After "Jimmy Mack," the group would have only two more Top 40 hits, both in 1967, and then they'd break up and then re-form, but it didn't change the fact that the hits had stopped coming; after 1972, they wouldn't chart again.

Martha Reeves still performs all over the world today, and looking back on their success—twenty-six chart hits, including two R&B #1s—it's obvious that the group was a major force in the recording industry during the 1960s. Yet it's that one controversial song, "Jimmy Mack," that came to be the song most appreciated by beach music lovers. It's safe to say that for them Vietnam never even entered the picture.

GENE McDANIELS

"A HUNDRED POUNDS OF CLAY"
1961, Billboard #3
Liberty 55308

T hat's absolutely true," Gene McDaniels said when I told him I'd read that he'd performed "A Hundred Pounds of Clay" just twice in the last five decades. "Right after it came out in 1961 I did Dick Clark and a bunch of shows, and I'd lip-sync the song. But singing it live? I only sang it live five or six times anyway—nightclub stuff, you know. But once I started writing, that all changed." Considering that most artists on this list spent the rest of their careers either looking for that next elusive hit record or performing those big charting songs from the past over and over again, Gene McDaniels is an anomaly. But despite the fact that his classic hit "A Hundred Pounds of Clay" is a beach music standard and that it was a Top 10 song as well, as a songwriter, music publisher and producer, he has had unparalleled success. The song is important for McDaniels for another reason, however; he says it taught him one of the most important lessons he learned in life.

Eugene McDaniels grew up in Omaha, Nebraska. He not only sang in the church choir but also formed his own gospel group when he was eleven. After graduating from college, he was working on the West Coast when he came to the attention of Liberty Records, with whom he signed in 1959. "I did an album conducted and produced by Johnny Mann of the Johnny Mann singers called *In Times Like These*—which was also my first single actually." That single and his next one did nothing, but his next, the 1961 classic "A Hundred Pounds of Clay," went very big. But at the time, McDaniels was more aware of the internal strife at Liberty than the song's potential.

"When I signed with them, Liberty Records was owned by Si Waronker, but after Si died Liberty was taken over by Al Bennet, a 'bean counter' for the company who was from Lubbock, Texas. There was also a guy in the mailroom from Lubbock, Snuff Garrett. He was a friend of Al's, and Al called him up from the mailroom to be the producer to the artists at Liberty Records. That's a helluva jump, from mailroom to head producer at Liberty! I was stunned by the fact that they had elevated this young guy to this position, and I didn't know that he had any musical background."

"Well, he had this song for me, 'A Hundred Pounds of Clay,' and he put this song together with the arrangers, and he was producing it, and he didn't like the way I was singing the song. So he asked me to clip the lyrics. Being a singer, and being very young, I was incensed by some guy from the mailroom telling me how to sing. I didn't understand; nobody explained to me that there's a specific sound out there that the audience wants to hear. He told me, 'You're singing too much, clip the lyrics.' I clipped them, and he thought I was responding angrily to his request. And I was! Well, he went to Al Bennet, who asked him, 'How'd he do?' and Snuff said, 'He blew it.' Al said, 'We're putting it out anyway. I'm not gonna spend $1,500 and not put this thing out.' So, he puts 'A Hundred Pounds of Clay' out, and it goes all the way to #3. We'll, it's egg on Snuff's face because he thought it was poorly done, and it's egg on my face because I wasn't performing to my ultimate ability. But it taught me a lesson, and that lesson is that you can always learn something. Snuff had a golden ear and produced Top 10 hits for a lot of Liberty artists."

"A Hundred Pounds of Clay" told the story of God creating the human race, and while it was a strange topic for a popular song, with backing vocals by the Johnny Mann singers and McDaniels's strong lead, the song shot up the charts and earned a gold record. But here the story takes an even stranger turn. In England, the BBC banned the song and wouldn't allow British radio stations to play it. The controversy arose not from the fact that it was a religious song, but instead the objection was that censors interpreted the song as suggesting women were created simply to be sexual beings, and the BBC felt this was blasphemous.

British pop singer Craig Douglas, who had already had a #1 hit with a cover of Sam Cooke's "Only Sixteen," was not about to miss an opportunity like that the banned record presented. Douglas decided to rewrite the "offensive" lyrics so they would pass the BBC censors, which resulted in the following changes: "He created a woman and a lots of lovin' for a man" became "He created old Adam then He made a woman for the man"; "For every kiss you're givin'" was changed to "For all the joy He's given"; "For the arms that are holdin' me tight" became "For my world full of beauty and life"; "Doin' just what he should do" was changed to "Makin' land and sky and sea"; and "To make a livin' dream like you" became "And doin' it all for you and me." Basically, the changes seemed to de-sex the woman in the song and dispel the idea that God would have created a being simply for man to love. Douglas knew how to work the censors, and he was given BBC approval to release the song and saw it soar to #9 on the British charts.

In America, McDaniels's next single, "A Tear," would go to #31 before he would finish 1961 with a third straight Top 40 song in "Tower of Strength," which would go to #5. The year 1962 followed the same successful pattern, and after "Chip Chip" (#10), four of his next five singles would make the Top 100. Although in just twenty months he had recorded and released eight Top 100 hits, between 1963 and 1967 he would release seven more singles and none of them would make the popular charts.

But this didn't worry McDaniels, because over time he had moved more into songwriting anyway. He not only wrote Les McCann's 1969 #1 jazz hit "Compared to What," but he also wrote 1974's "Feel Like Making Love," which was recorded by Roberta Flack, went to #1 and earned platinum status and a Grammy Award. McDaniels later won a BMI award for the song, which had more than five million airplays by the 1980s.

For all of McDaniels's success, what stands out most in the minds of beach music lovers is "A Hundred Pounds of Clay." McDaniels is pleased that the song has been well received in Carolina beach music circles, though he thinks the most important thing about it is the life lesson he learned at the time. "Life is different every day, and sometimes your enemy is your best friend. I've been looking for Snuff Garrett to ask him to forgive me for my attitude during those times. I was a kid—I didn't know what I was doing. I have great respect for him now. He got hit records from all of the Liberty artists, and it was amazing. I'm now probably one of his biggest fans. He doesn't know that, but I've tried to find him to tell him thanks. He set me up in a way that everybody was paying attention, and then he got me two more Top 10 songs. That really helped because when I started writing people took me seriously."

While McDaniels knows the song taught him an important lesson in life, and the BBC found it blasphemous, beach music lovers simply think "A Hundred Pounds of Clay" is an incredible song and one of the all-time great classics.

STICK McGHEE

"DRINKIN' WINE SPO-DEE-O-DEE"
1949, pre-Billboard
Atlantic 873

S tick" McGhee was not a drummer, as some might think given his nickname, but a guitar player and a singer. His nickname wasn't "Sticks," plural, either, but "Stick." "Stick" was born Granville McGhee and got his nickname by pushing his polio-stricken brother Walter ("Brownie") McGhee around in a wagon with a stick. Perhaps it doesn't really matter all that much, because anyone who can turn out a rollicking song such as "Drinkin' Wine Spo-dee-o-dee" deserves attention no matter what he's called.

Before World War II, McGhee was already working toward a career in the music business, playing smaller venues and working up his guitar-playing act. He entered the army in 1942, and after his discharge in 1946, McGhee, along with brother Brownie and friend Dan Burley, laid down a track Stick used to sing in the army, retitled "Drinkin' Wine Spo-dee-o-dee," on the small Harlem label. (Spo-dee-o-dee is reported to be the leftovers and dregs of many wine bottles, poured together and passed around.) However, Stick's army version had been quite different and quite profane ("Drinkin' wine m***** f****r, G*d**n!"). Obviously that wasn't going to be allowed on the radio, so the cleaned-up version was released. It went nowhere, probably due to the fact that the Harlem version still wasn't the fast track listeners today are familiar with; it was much slower and much less of a rocker. However, one of the men who would establish Atlantic Records, Ahmet Ertegun, had heard the song and liked it, so in February 1949 he had Stick, with Brownie on guitar and "Big Chief" Ellis on piano, rerecord it with a new uptempo rhythm. Recorded on Atlantic 873 and backed with "Blues Mixture (I'd Rather Drink Muddy Water)," the record was Atlantic's first big hit, going all the way to #3 on the R&B charts.

McGhee continued to record for Atlantic, turning out songs such as "Drank Up All the Wine Last Night" and "One Monkey Don't Stop No Show," but he was never able to match the success of that first hit. He eventually ended up at King, where he cut such living-on-the-edge singles as "Whiskey, Women and Loaded Dice," "Double Crossin' Liquor," "Dealin' from the Bottom" and others, but still no hits followed. After a brief stint at Savoy, McGhee retired from music in 1960; in 1961, he died from cancer.

"Drinkin Wine Spo-dee-o-dee" has been one of the most often covered records on this survey, having been done by artists as diversified as Jerry Lee Lewis, Wynonie Harris and Kid Rock. Its party-time feel makes it a classic for the ages and a popular beach music rocker as well.

BOB MEYER
AND THE RIVIERAS

"BEHOLD"
1964, did not chart
Casino 103/Lawn 238

B ob Meyer and the Rivieras had a smooth sound, so much so that they are usually tagged as a "blue-eyed soul" group, as are artists such as the Righteous Brothers, Dusty Springfield, Hall and Oates and others. That's not bad company to be in, and their shining moment in the beach music world, 1964's "Behold," is a perfect example of why that label is so fitting.

They originated in Charlotte, North Carolina, where teenagers Nat Speir and Charles Van Wagner formed the group in 1958. The 1958 lineup also included Joe Harris, Smitty Flynn, Bill Bolen and Dwight Stephens, and though the lineup would vary greatly over the ensuing years, it was the addition of new lead vocalist Bob Meyer in 1963 that allowed the group to really find their sound. The addition of Meyer's name to the group may have been welcome as well, for in 1964 the Indiana group the Rivieras would have a hit with "California Sun," so the name change lessened the confusion.

No one who heard the group's soulful "Behold," written by Meyer and Speir and released in 1964, would confuse it with anything done by the "other" Rivieras, however. Produced by Harry Karras, who would also later produce the Swingin' Medallions' "Double Shot," the tune acquired an instant audience along the East Coast and was not only released on the Casino label but also saw subsequent release on the slightly more prestigious Lawn label, a subsidiary of Swan. Swan, of course, was the label where the Beatles had previously gone to #1 with "She Loves You," and perhaps through the connection between the two labels, legend has it that the Beatles heard and liked "Behold" and even considered recording it for a while. That idea is not as far-fetched as it might seem, for in 1963 and '64 the group had covered American soul classics such as "Money," "Please Mr. Postman," "You Really Got a Hold on Me" and "Anna." By late 1964, however, Lennon and McCartney had come into their own as songwriters and had essentially quit doing covers, which may have led to them changing their minds about recording "Behold."

Neither the Lawn nor Casino release charted, though the flip side, "You've Got to Tell Me," would later go on to be a Northern Soul classic; in fact, in England the 45 is highly collectible today for the flip and not "Behold." The group would go on to record a number of singles such as "My Girl Stormy" (1965), "Caring for You" (1967) and "I Only Get This Feeling" (1968) on a variety of labels, but that big chart hit would always remain elusive. There would continue to be many personnel changes throughout the '60s until the group folded in 1970.

While many groups in this book had at least their allotted fifteen minutes of fame if nothing else, Bob Meyer and the Rivieras didn't quite get there. Still, "Behold" is a well-known and well-loved beach music classic and one that has played on countless jukeboxes throughout the South.

GARNET MIMMS AND
THE ENCHANTERS

"A QUIET PLACE"
1964, Billboard #78
United Artists 715

Like many famous frontmen, Garnet Mimms didn't stay with his backing group, the Enchanters, throughout his career. But what's interesting in this case is that even when the label named the Enchanters as Mimms's backing group, they sometimes weren't, and when they named Mimms as a solo act, he sometimes wasn't. In fact, the group actually cut just three records together, and the best of these is the beach classic "A Quiet Place."

Like many R&B musicians, Garnet Mimms had a strong background in the church and gospel music. Early on, he sang with several groups, and after a stint in the military he started the Philadelphia-based group the Gainors in 1958. The group's first recording, 1958's doo-wopper "The Secret," was a regional hit, and Cameo picked up and released the first two Gainors' regional recordings hoping for a little national chart action that was nevertheless elusive. The Gainors had a few more singles before Mimms left to form another group, Garnet Mimms and the Enchanters. The Enchanters were Sam Bell (from the Gainors), Charles Boyer and Zola Pearnell, and the group moved to New York and signed with United Artists.

But almost from the start, the Enchanters weren't always the group backing up Mimms on those Garnet Mimms and the Enchanters singles, despite what the record label said. For example, on "Cry Baby," the group's biggest single, which went all the way to #4 in 1963 and reportedly sold more than one million copies, the actual backing group was the

Gospelaires, whose members included Dionne Warwick and Dee Dee Warwick. On the flip side of the record, however, "Don't Change Your Heart," it was indeed the Enchanters singing backup. "Baby Don't You Weep" (#30) and a cover of the Impressions' "For Your Precious Love" (#26) both made the Top 40, though the singles billed as just "Garnet Mimms," sans Enchanters, "Tell Me Baby" (#69) and "One Girl" (#67), did not. On the flip side of "One Girl" the real Enchanters *were* billed and *were* singing backup on the beach music classic, 1964's "A Quiet Place." Mimms's wailing song of a man who "can't get no sleep, on this noisy street" is the beach song with perhaps the three most famous opening words—"Johnny, Johnny Dollar"—of all time. As a national record, it only went to #78, so it was not a big performer for the band.

Despite the confusion over who was and was not singing backup, the group was off to a good start, but perhaps the question over whether this was a one-man show or not led to Mimms decisively going out on his own in 1964 right after "A Quiet Place" charted. The Enchanters stayed together, but without Mimms they didn't seem to have the magic, and they folded in 1966. Mimms, meanwhile, continued to record, sometimes using the Enchanters as uncredited backup singers. With his wide vocal range and wailing soul style, he remained a hot act over the next few years. He cut eight more records for United Artists, though only three charted, and only one, "I'll Take Good Care of You" (#30), broke the Top 40. After his career as a solo artist appeared to have peaked, he worked with Jimi Hendrix in 1967. By the early '70s, Mimms found that he was still very popular on the growing UK Northern Soul scene, so he moved to England and continued to record well into the 1970s.

Today, many people may be most familiar with his work through covers such as "Cry Baby" by Janis Joplin. However, to legions of beach music fans, the haunting words "Johnny, Johnny Dollar" can only mean the onset of one of the greatest beach tunes.

THE MOB

"I Dig Everything About You"
1971, Billboard #83
Colossus 130

H ere Gary Beisbier and I were, young guys right out of Chicago, living
in LA and dating Playboy Bunnies," MOB founding member James
Holvay told me in an interview. "My girlfriend and I were living in an
apartment, a half block up from the Whiskey A Go Go. It overlooked all of
Los Angeles, and at night, it was a pretty awesome sight. It doesn't get any
better than that, and it didn't. Did all that play a part of the writing process
of 'I Dig Everything About You'? My guess would be yes, it did," Holvay
said. And while as a Billboard Top 100 musical entity the MOB had just
a couple of Top 100 hits, as a Chicago favorite and as writers of songs for
other artists, the MOB was a powerful musical force indeed.

The Chicago-based MOB was one of the first horn bands and actually
predated similar groups such as the Spiral Starecase, Chicago and Blood,
Sweat and Tears. The band had a strong regional following during the
1960s, and the band's leaders, James Holvay and Gary Beisbier, had been a
part of a group known as the Livers that had cut the single "Beatle Time"
in 1963. After the Livers, Holvay and Beisbier formed the MOB with Al
Herrera, Tony Nedza, Bobby Ruffino, James Franz and Michael Sistak.
As for the group's name, Holvay says, "I was watching the late, late, late
show one Friday night and an old movie came on called *The MOB*, made
in about 1953. The whole vision came to me. I thought, 'What a perfect
name for group. A bunch of guys with pinstripe suits, black shirts, white ties,

The MOB in the 1960s. *Courtesy of Al Schrank and Al Herrera.*

carnations, white suspenders and spats, playing R&B music. Horn section, B3 organ, high energy, dancing, choreography. It's never been done. Hell, we could become bigger than the Beatles.' I actually thought that. We all thought that." Though they released a number of singles between 1966 and 1968, none of them charted, and their dreams of success comparable to the Beatles did not materialize. In fact, "we even went dormant for a year or so," Holvay said.

Although their own singles were stiffing, at the same time Beisbier and Holvay were writing music for another Chicago-based band, the Buckinghams, and those songs were taking the national charts by storm. Holvay's song for the Buckinghams, "Kind of a Drag," hit #1, and Holvay and Beisbier together wrote "Don't You Care" (#6), "Hey Baby (They're Playing Our Song)" (#12) and "Susan" (#11), which were all chart hits. As a result, Biesber's and Holvay's writing helped crosstown rivals the Buckinghams earn Billboard's title of "The Most Listened to Band in America" in 1967, while other than locals very few people were familiar with the MOB at all.

But big changes were in store for the MOB, and they made a few alterations and developed their act into more of a Vegas-style club band sound. Holvay said that at one performance, "while playing at the Americana Hotel in Puerto Rico, Jerry Ross, owner and producer for Colossus records, happened to come into the lounge on his last day of his vacation before flying back to Philly." Ross liked what he heard from the group, and he quickly signed them to his stable of artists. "Having been on four record labels and having seen other horn bands and the Buckinghams rack up hits, we were elated to even be recording with any record label. Colossus had a few hits under their belt, so we thought that this would finally be our ticket to success." In fact, the fledgling Colossus label had recently released Top 10 hits such as "Venus" (#1) by Shocking Blue and "Ma Belle Amie" (#5) by the Tee Set, and it seemed to follow that the new sound, the proven writing ability and the up-and-coming label were the perfect recipe for success and the MOB was about to break big.

First they needed a song, but fortunately, Holvay and Beisbier had never had a problem coming up with hits. "Our girlfriends had an off night from work at the Playboy Club, and we were all going to go out to dinner together. Gary and his girl came over to our apartment to pick us up. Gary and I were sitting in the living room, and a week or so earlier I'd come up with the verse, 'Baby I need your sweet, sweet lovin', baby. Ooo baby.' That's all I had. I got out my acoustic guitar and played it for Gary. He said, 'Hey—I like that—I've got an idea.' I handed him the guitar, and he wrote the chorus. Songwriters say that the really good songs just flow out naturally—you don't struggle with it. We probably wrote that song in fifteen minutes." The song was, of course, "I Dig Everything About You," now a beach music classic.

Surprisingly—especially given Holvay and Beisbier's track record as writers—the song really didn't do much on the charts. Holvay was shocked, especially since of all the hit songs he'd written, "I'd say that 'I Dig Everything About You' is on the top of my list" as a personal favorite. But soon the problem came to light. "Unbeknownst to us, Jerry Ross was having financial difficulties at the time. Radio stations were playing the record, but after hearing the song our fans were going to the stores to buy the record and lo and behold...no records in the rack. The way you move up on the radio station rotation playlist and get more spins every hour is that the station calls the local record stores in the area every week and asks how many singles were sold. As you sell more records, they increase your airplay. No record sales, you move down on the playlist. Watching that happen just killed me. I was heartbroken. Had I known then what I know now, I would've been on the phone hourly, screaming at Jerry to get records in the stores. I would've driven to the record distributor or pressing plant and taken the records to the stores myself, just to keep that airplay going." Despite its superior quality, the song peaked nationally at #83 on the Billboard charts.

Their next single, "Give It to Me," went a little higher, peaking at #71 in 1971, but these were their only charting records, and the magic that Holvay and Beisbier had worked so well for the Buckinghams seemed, once again, to have eluded their own group. Colossus, too, had peaked, and in fact the MOB's records were the label's last charters; Colossus folded by

The MOB in the 1970s. *Courtesy of Al Schrank and Al Herrera.*

1971 after pressing fewer than 150 singles. For Holvay, it was a bitter disappointment: "Had we signed with a major label and found a producer who was able to capture who we were early in the game, I feel like we would've had a handful of major hits. But Colossus didn't have the money or the marketing machine behind it to bring the records home." After the collapse of Colossus and after having cut just four singles and one album, the group tried a few different labels but had no further chart success.

"I Dig Everything About You" is like many other top beach music hits: a great song that didn't make much of a splash nationally but is nevertheless a big sound embraced by beach music lovers everywhere. "It's amazing, and it always blows my mind when I hear that 'I Dig Everything About You,' or any MOB song for that matter, is appreciated by anyone, especially after all these years," Holvay told me. "When you write a song and are lucky enough to get it released on a record label, you hope that someone, first of all, even hears it, and second of all, likes it." Given its placement here, it's another one of those records beach music listeners see as compelling evidence that they have the ability to recognize a quality cut even if no one else can.

THE MONZAS

"HEY! I KNOW YOU"
1964, did not chart
Wand 1120

N elson Miller wrote the song on a porch in Ocean Drive," Monzas member Linda "Quig" Quinlan James told me in an interview for this book, "and I helped with a word here and there." How appropriate that one of the greatest beach songs to come out of the Carolinas was written at the beach, and not just any beach, but in many ways *the* beach, the place often considered the home of beach music. For a while there in the mid-1960s, the Monzas' "Hey! I Know You" was blaring out of every jukebox in Ocean Drive and from Florida to Virginia and all points in between.

The Monzas were formed when UNC student Nelson "Salty" Miller decided to put together a band and enlisted the help of drummer Ward May. As the band came together, they added pianist Bing Greeson and then singer Skippy Hinshaw. Hinshaw had a sister named Sharon who had a friend named Linda "Quig" Quinlan, and the girls would occasionally come out to hear the band practice. On one occasion, they were asked to provide backing vocals for a song the group was practicing, and after that the guys took the bold and almost unprecedented step of adding female members to their lineup (though the girls were just sixteen at the time). It was a good move, because Linda and Sharon's vocal contributions make those Monzas tunes some of the most unique sounds in the beach music catalogue.

Adding Linda also brought about another benefit—indirectly, at least, she was responsible for the group's name. Linda drove a Corvair Monza Spider,

The Monzas. *Courtesy of Linda Quinlan James.*

and she said that as "there were many other bands with car names at the time, my friend Rodney Carden suggested the name Monzas and it stuck." So starting in 1962, the Monzas toured the Carolinas making their own special brand of beach music. But their really big break came when they recorded "Hey! I Know You."

"There were two cuts of 'Hey! I Know You,'" James said. "The first was done at Copeland Studios in Greensboro, and the second was done in Charlotte at the Arthur Smith Studios" about a year later. "The first cut was much faster than the second, but there were no major differences other than that one was faster than the other." With Mickey Combs singing lead and Linda and Sharon's haunting backing voices, "Hey! I Know You" was picked up for national release by the Wand label. According to James, what really gave the record a boost was the playtime it received from DJ Charlie Brown (Ed Weiss) of WKIX radio in Raleigh. "Charlie Brown was very instrumental in the song going as far as it did. Back in the day, WKIX was a huge and very popular radio station. He played it a lot and told other DJs about it." And though the record never did much nationally, regionally it was a bona fide hit.

The Monzas. *Courtesy of Linda Quinlan James.*

The group didn't have any more national releases after "Hey! I Know You," though "we had other records on Pacific," Linda said. The group's lineup would continue to change, however, despite the fact that it appeared they had at least taken a small step toward the big time. Sharon left the group in 1965, and although Linda had stayed on as the only female in the group after Sharon's departure, she, too, left in 1968. The guys kept recording as the Monzas, and other members were added (and subtracted), but they were never again able to equal the magic of "Hey! I Know You." It's a song that has remained a beach music favorite now for decades.

"I am still surprised every time I hear it on the radio, especially up here in Virginia," Linda says. "I might have gotten tired of singing it at one time, but it still gives me cold chills when I perform it or hear it." It is a record that has clearly stood the test of time.

BOBBY MOORE AND
THE RHYTHM ACES

"SEARCHING FOR MY LOVE"
1966, Billboard #27
Checker 1129

W e were playing the song in clubs for a long time before we ever recorded
it. We went to Muscle Shoals and were one of the first Chess groups
to record there. We cut the record, and it took off," Bobby Moore Jr. told me.
The song in question is Bobby Moore and the Rhythm Aces' "Searching for
My Love," a classic rhythm and blues tune of the "begging and pleading"
type. Chico Jenkins's plaintive vocal conveys a sense of loss far better than
many songs designed to impart a very similar message. Despite the fact that
the tune was a sizable hit, the group was never able to sustain any long-term
chart success, but even with their limited output they did manage to leave
beach music lovers with an undisputed classic.

Bobby Moore's first experience in a band came when he was serving in
the army in the early 1950s. A tenor sax player, his first band consisted of
members of the Fort Benning, Georgia army marching band. After leaving
the army, he decided to make music his profession and formed the Rhythm
Aces in 1961. When the group's lineup solidified, "there were six of us: Dad,
me, Chico Jenkins, Joe Frank, Clifford Laws and John Baldwin," Moore
said. As a unit, the Rhythm Aces quickly gained a reputation as a first-class
ensemble, and as a result, they had the opportunity to back up singers such
as Ray Charles, Sam and Dave, Etta James, Kim Weston, Wilson Pickett,
Sam Cooke and Otis Redding.

Bobby Moore and the Rhythm Aces. *Courtesy of Bobby Moore Jr.*

They didn't want to be just a backup band, however, and in 1965, they got their first real shot as a feature act at the legendary Muscle Shoals studio in Alabama. There they recorded the now legendary "Searching for My Love," which Moore himself had written. "We'd been performing it for a while, and Dad and Chico decided it would be a good one to record because people liked it when we were playing it in clubs—I think the response there had a lot to do with it." The record executives at Chess Records in Chicago heard the tune and responded positively as well and, after acquiring the rights, released it on their Checker label in 1966. The group watched the song soar into the Top 40 before finally settling in at #27, where it reportedly sold more than one million copies. The benefits of having a hit record were immediately obvious, Moore said: "Before the record came out, we had been making like $25 to $30 a night, and after the record, we were making $300 a night." They even performed on television's *Where the Action Is* as a follow-up to the single and were hoping their next release would sustain that momentum. That release, the equally impressive (for beach music lovers, at least) "Try My Love Again," "didn't do that much though," Moore says, peaking at

#97, while their next single, 1967's "Chained to Your Heart," did not make the Top 100 at all, though it did make the R&B charts. Despite the promise shown by their first three singles, Checker didn't seem to have much faith in the group's ability to produce long term, and after they released one more non-charting single, Checker dropped them from the label.

"Dad kept the band going even after the label released us, and we have been playing for four decades now," Moore said. "Dad was a class act, and today I'm still trying to carry on the legacy." Though with only four singles, only one of which made it big on the charts, the group's legacy has indeed endured on the strength of the great "Searching for My Love," a song that beach music lovers consider far and away to be a solid classic.

LENNY O'HENRY

"ACROSS THE STREET"
1964, Billboard #98
Atco 6291

In terms of success, the songs and artists in this book are a mixed bag. For example, many of these artists were very successful, although their songs on this list may or may not have been hits. Other artists are not so well known outside of the beach music scene, but their songs may have been hits for a moment. Then there are those that were big "beach bands," so at least along the East Coast we know about them even if no one else does. Then there is Lenny O'Henry, the man who gave us the classic "Across the Street."

Lenny O'Henry's real name was Danny Cannon, and initially, as a member of the Vibra-Harps in the late 1950s, he worked under his own name with group members Donnie Elbert, Charles Hargro and Donald Simmons. The Vibra-Harps recorded a few failed platters for Beech, Fury and Atco before Cannon—now taking the name Lenny O'Henry—set out on his own and recorded "Cheated Heart" in 1961 for ABC-Paramount and "Mr. Moonlight" for Smash in 1963. His next record, "Across the Street," was recorded on Atco in 1963 and released in 1964, and it brought O'Henry his fleeting moment in the spotlight. Despite superior production by Bob Crewe and an arrangement by Charlie Calello, both of Four Seasons' hits fame, the single stalled at #98 and the next week was right back off the charts. After cutting a couple more singles for Atco—"Sweet Young Love" in 1964 and "Saturday Angel" in 1967—O'Henry was done and faded into the background forever.

The Classic Years

In his book *The Heart of Rock & Soul: The 1001 Greatest Singles Ever Made*, rock critic Dave Marsh lists "Across the Street" at #782—not a bad all-time listing for a record that just barely dented the Hot 100 and then for just a week. Marsh notes that the record's appeal lies in O'Henry's unexplained banishment from the party across the street where his girl is "dancin' and romancin'" and his mournful promise to get her and "love her so she'll never return." The sound, the soul, the words and the mood all make "Across the Street" a song that beach music lovers have appreciated far more than radio listeners initially did in 1964. That would make it their loss.

THE O'KAYSIONS

"GIRL WATCHER"
1968, Billboard #5
ABC11094

We used to play down at Atlantic Beach a lot, and when we got back home people would say, 'Did you meet any girls this weekend?'" O'Kaysions founder Wayne Pittman told the author. "I'd say, 'I didn't meet any, but I sure do like to watch them.'" It was from this simple concept that "Girl Watcher," the O'Kaysions' 1968 million-selling hit, was born. "Girl Watcher" is all the better because like "Under the Boardwalk," "Washed Ashore," "Sand in My Shoes" and "Summertime's Calling Me," it is one of those "beach music about the beach" songs, and as a result, it is truly one of the great classics of the genre.

The O'Kaysions started in Wilson, North Carolina, in the '60s as the Kays, though by 1968 Donnie Weaver, Wayne Pittman, Ron Turner, Jim Spiedel, Jimmy Hinnant and Bruce Joyner had changed their name to the O'Kaysions because "in order to play in the clubs up north, you had to become a union member," Pittman said. "You had to register your band's name, and there was a DJ in New York named Murray the K, and we couldn't register our name because it was too similar to his. So we coined the name O'Kaysions so we could try to maintain our identity in North and South Carolina, Georgia and Virginia where we played, so people would still know who we were."

Their first recording under the new name was "Girl Watcher," the Pittman-penned tune they would record for the tiny NorthState label in 1968.

The O'Kaysions. *Courtesy of Wayne Pittman.*

According to Pittman, after his comment about liking to watch girls, one of the band members said, "'Wayne, you're the writer, why don't you write a song called "I'm a Girl Watcher."' What was funny was that about a month before, I had written a tune and I hadn't even thought about putting any words to it yet. But when he made that comment, it was like a lightbulb went off in my head. I said, 'Okay, I will, I'll go back and write it, and I'll be back next week,' and that's exactly what I did. I wrote it in two nights that week. There was this great-looking girl that ran by my house every afternoon after work, and I'd be at home, and she'd go by when I was writing. That helped a lot too."

The catchy tune, which seemed to precisely mirror the thoughts and pastimes of many a young man in the Carolinas and especially along the coast, was played regionally almost nonstop, and it sold very well. Soon the record came to the attention of ABC Records, which decided to pick up distribution. They liked the song and decided to release it exactly as it had been recorded. (This fact apparently led to a legendary story that someone at NorthState had lost the master tapes and so the ABC single had to be dubbed from the original 45, but Pittman says it isn't true. "The ABC people flew down from New York, met the owners of NorthState and took the tapes back. They had and still have the master tapes.") The song did well, going to #5 on the charts, and eventually it reached gold record status with one million sales by December 1968. An album followed, and the group seemed to be on their way.

The album actually had some good cuts on it, but unfortunately it was uneven because "ABC wanted something quick and something fast, and we had to do the whole album in two days. It just wasn't a good product." Though "Love Machine" did chart at #76, nothing else the group recorded registered, and Pittman believes this may have been partly due to Atlanta promoter Bill Lowery. "The North State people thought they had the right to sign us to any booking agency they wanted to. They signed us with Lowery without our knowledge, and he was supposed to book us, and this was even before 'Girl Watcher' charted. But Lowery just wasn't booking us enough, and we cancelled our agreement with him. We then signed with Associated Booking in New York City. Well, Lowery had a lot of power and contacts in the industry, and the word we got was that he put the kiss of death on us. So we promoted the record and made it a hit, but ABC wouldn't put a lot of money behind us after that." Consequently, after a couple of little-heard singles on ABC and then a couple on Cotillion, by the early 1970s the group was done.

Eventually, Pittman decided it was time to get out of the music business. "That period was the beginning of the psychedelic and acid rock scene, and 'Girl Watcher' had been an anomaly. Everywhere we played, the acid rock groups would go on, with all the noise and distortion, and there were the drugs all around, and I just didn't want to go in that direction. I knew I'd burn myself out if I stayed in it, so I just stopped performing." But the music business changed a good bit for the better over the next decade ("Disco kind of cleaned the music up," he says), so by the 1980s he had re-formed the group. The O'Kaysions are active to this day and perform throughout the South playing the big beach sound.

"I knew 'Girl Watcher' would be big on a long-term basis, because of the nature of the song. It was a happy song," he says. Indeed it is, and the timeless "Girl Watcher" is a song known to millions and always a crowd pleaser, even all these years later.

PATTY AND THE EMBLEMS

"MIXED UP, SHOOK UP, GIRL"
1964, Billboard #37
Herald 590

Listening to Patty and the Emblems' "Mixed Up, Shook Up, Girl" today, it boggles the mind to try and account for the fact that not only was this their one and only Top 40 hit but it didn't place particularly high in the Top 40 either. They had the sound and the talent, but for whatever reason, listeners never again warmed to a Patty and the Emblems single.

Patty and the Emblems were a New Jersey act formed by lead singer Patty Russell, backed by Eddie Watts, Vance Walker and Alexander Wildes. As anyone who has ever heard "Mixed Up, Shook Up, Girl" would attest, Russell had a strong voice on par with any of the lead singers of the major girl groups popular at the time, and the Emblems were first-rate backup singers as well. Add songwriter Leon Huff to the mix, and it would seem to have been a recipe for a long line of hits for the group. Huff and partner Kenny Gamble would eventually go on to be one of the most popular songwriting teams in the world and would write "Cowboys to Girls" for the Intruders, "Love Train" and "Backstabbers" for the O'Jays, "Only the Strong Survive" for Jerry Butler and many, many more.

In 1964, however, Huff was still more or less unknown, so when he wrote "Mixed Up, Shook Up, Girl" it was not as an established songwriter. In fact, the Patty and the Emblems song was his very first Top 40 record. The song went to #37 on the charts, but considering it was also the very first recording for Patty and the Emblems, the future looked bright indeed.

But whereas Huff would go on to years of unparalleled success, unfortunately, the group seemed to have already had their fifteen minutes of fame. Their next two releases were 1964's "The Sound of Music Makes Me Want to Dance" (another Huff-penned tune) and "And We Danced," and neither record did anything, nor did a couple of the flip sides Huff had written. Future singles by the group all went nowhere. Like many '60s soul artists, their work actually found more of a following in England on the Northern Soul scene, and Kev Roberts ranks their 1968 single "I'm Gonna Love You a Long, Long Time" as the #38 record on his Top 500 Northern Soul records of all time.

Eventually, Patty Russell left the music business and got married, and the group dispersed and went its separate ways. Perhaps the group's failure to chart again had something to do with their sound, because listening to their music—the songs listed above as well as some of the others they recorded—one gets the sense they never really found an identity, as groups such as the Shirelles and Chiffons did. All of their songs sound very different from one another, and maybe record buyers were looking for a definable consistency that the group's records simply didn't offer. For whatever reason, Patty and the Emblems' one hit would classify them for all time as a one-hit wonder, even if that hit was a beach music classic.

FREDA PAYNE

"BAND OF GOLD"
1970, Billboard #3
Invictus 9075

To be honest, I thought the lyrics were a little strange," Freda Payne said, laughing, when I asked her about "Band of Gold." "I mean, why would a young girl on her wedding night want to stay in another room? The lyrics say 'that night on our honeymoon/we stayed in separate rooms.' What's up with that?" Despite Payne's reservations about the lyrics, "Band of Gold" would make her a superstar, and as she says, "It really turned my career around."

Detroit native Freda Payne garnered her first acclaim as an entertainer by winning several amateur contests singing in her early teens, and her talent brought her to the attention of a young Berry Gordy. "I first met Berry when I was around fourteen," Payne told me. "When you mention the name Berry Gordy Jr., you think of a pioneer in the recording industry, Motown founder and a very prosperous man. But back then Berry didn't have substantial funding or a record company, just a lot of ambition to manage artists and to get his own record label." But Gordy was aware of Payne's talent and wanted to sign her to a contract. "Berry had seen me on television on Ed Mckenzie's *Dance Hour*, Detroit's equivalent to *American Bandstand*. The show had teenagers dancing to top records, and he also had guests who would perform a couple of songs—Sammy Davis Jr., Della Reese, the Four Freshman, people like that. I'd also been singing with the Jimmy Wilkins Orchestra, and I'd been singing on the radio on Don Large's *Makeway for Youth* show. So Berry heard about me, and that drew his attention to me."

Gordy wrote some songs for Payne, and "he took me into a studio which was called United Sound. We recorded the songs, and then he, my mother and I all drove to New York. He wanted to get a deal on Roulette records, and because he got a positive response he wanted to sign me to a managerial contract. My mother, who was not a pushover, was not receptive—they couldn't agree on terms. I think had he been more modest in his demands she would have said okay." So she continued to perform locally, and when she was eighteen she moved to New York and signed a record deal with ABC-Paramount. But it wasn't until she was exposed to the magic of former Motown songwriters and producers Holland-Dozier-Holland that she achieved that much-anticipated stardom. "In 1968, a friend called me and said 'an old friend of yours from Detroit, Brian Holland, is sitting here with me and he wants you to come over.' I had gone to high school with Brian, but by that time they had become Holland-Dozier-Holland and were famous. When I got there, he asked me if I was under contract or anything. Well as it happened my contract was just up with ABC, and so was my management contract, so I was literally free of any contractual obligations. So Brian said, 'Would you like to come with us? We just left Motown and formed our own label called Invictus.' I flew to Detroit and that was it."

Her second single for Invictus was "Band of Gold," and though she thought the lyrics were strange it didn't deter her. "It wasn't that I didn't want to do the song—I was going to do it whether I liked it or not. I just told them, 'This is for a fifteen-year-old or something—it's so immature,'" she laughed. "But you know, I think those lyrics actually drew more interest to the song.

The song benefitted not only from Payne's dynamic vocals and the writing of Holland-Dozier-Holland but also from the presence of Motown's famous Funk Brothers on backup, the then relatively unknown Ray Parker Jr. on lead guitar and backups Joyce Wilson and Telma Hopkins, both of whom would be the "Dawn" in Tony Orlando and Dawn less than a year later. Also, Payne's sister Scherrie and several members of the Originals were there, so it was a veritable who's who of talent in the studio. It all paid off, as "Band of Gold" climbed to #3 on the Billboard charts and went to #1 in the UK. "My career took off," Payne said. "I started getting requests for interviews, getting booked on TV shows, my salary went up, everything was suddenly better." "Band of Gold" was followed by a number of Invictus singles, the highest-charting being "Bring the Boys Home," which reached #12 in 1971. She continued to record, but at the same time with her considerable talent she diversified and branched out into television, movies and Broadway too.

Over the years she has hosted her own television show, *Today's Black Woman*, acted in movies and recently appeared on *American Idol*. "Regardless of what else I've done, I was educated on a musical basis by singing standards and jazz and show tunes, so what sustained me after the hit records faded out was the fact that I could still work and do other things like Broadway and theater. I've reinvented myself. But 'Band of Gold' started all that."

Obviously Freda Payne hardly needs the acclaim of having a great beach single on this list, but nevertheless "Band of Gold" is considered one of the greatest Carolina beach music classics. For all her accolades, she considers its placement on this list "a real honor."

THE PLATTERS

"I Love You 1,000 Times"
1966, Billboard #31
Musicor 1166

"With This Ring"
1967, Billboard #14
Musicor 1229

"Washed Ashore (On a Lonely Island in the Sea)"
1967, Billboard #56
Musicor 1251

We felt the change coming," Platters lead singer Sonny Turner told me. "The Beatles hit and then they had Motown, and we felt the whole format of the rhythm and blues era was changing. The soul mixed with the R&B and pop music—the writers were beginning to combine the sounds. The music scene was shifting." This meant that in order to survive, the Platters would have to change too, and no matter how successful they had been, those '50s-style hits simply weren't going to work in the '60s. So they changed labels and changed their sound, and the result was three monster hits, all behind the big voice of lead singer Sonny Turner—the beach classics "With This Ring," "Washed Ashore" and "I Love You 1,000 Times."

Like the Drifters, the Platters were one of those groups that had a fluctuating lineup, and as a result, different groups recorded different hits in very distinct periods. Unlike the Drifters, the Platters really only had two lead singers, which basically broke down to Tony Williams in the '50s and Sonny Turner in the '60s. Though during both periods the group and their different lead singers produced quality work, it's the work from Turner's time as frontman that is most listened to today by beach music fans. Before Turner came on board, in the 1950s the Platters had Tony Williams, David Lynch, Herb Reed, Alex Robi and Zola Taylor. This lineup

The Platters. *Courtesy of Sonny Turner.*

cut a number of early singles, and while none of them really did much on the charts, "Only You" did make some noise regionally. After Mercury picked the single up and released the record nationally, it soared to #5, and their next single, "The Great Pretender," became their first #1 hit. With Williams on lead, between 1955 and 1960 the group churned out some of the greatest hits of the early rock-and-roll era, including "My Prayer" (#1, 1956), "Twilight Time" (#1, 1958), "Smoke Gets in Your Eyes"(#1, 1958) and many, many more.

Like many acts, the continued success as a group wasn't enough to keep all of the members happy, and lead singer Tony Williams decided to go out on his own. After Williams left, manager Buck Ram brought in Sonny Turner as the group's new lead, but as the group tried to weather the departure of other key members over the next few years the hits stopped coming, and by 1963 their records were no longer even making the charts. Mercury seemed determined, however, to keep trying to have them do the same type of material that had worked for them in the '50s, and for a while it looked like the Platters were destined to become just another oldies act.

But the group wasn't going to go down without a fight, and Turner had the voice and charisma to make it all work again. With Turner, Lynch and Reed, along with new members Nate Nelson and Sandra Dawn, the group reinvented itself to adapt to the changing music scene. They left Mercury in 1965 and went to Musicor, where in 1966 they released the smooth and soulful "I Love You 1,000 Times." "Inez Foxx and Luther Dixon came up with 'I Love You 1,000 Times,'" Turner told me. "They felt we needed another hit, and they asked Buck to give it me." The group worked on the song, though initially not everyone agreed on how the song should be sung. Luther Dixon told Turner, "'Just sing it like you feel it,' but Buck wanted me to sing it a different way. Luther said, 'Buck, you're thinking old school, old fashioned, the music's changing—Sonny has a feel for it—let him sing it the way he feels it.' So I sang it my way and from the heart. Afterward, Luther told me, 'That's it—you nailed it.' And sure enough—bam!—hit record."

Interestingly enough, the version of the song most beach music fans know and love was not the original 45 version but is the version reissued on oldies 45s and the albums. Even without the lines

Love notes I treasured
Loving you was not a sin
Punishment was pleasure
Oh I'd do it all over again

I wrote and I wrote til my fingers got sore
I had to write just a little bit more
Cause I love you, I love you
Girl I love you, I love you
I love you 1,000 times

the single version of the song reached #31 on the charts and was the group's first hit in years. A couple of releases later, 1967's "With This Ring" was another bona fide hit. "Richard 'Popcorn' Wylie came up with 'With This Ring,' and this was yet another move toward that new sound," Turner said. "On this song I came into my own—I didn't have to mimic Tony Williams. We wanted a brassy song and sound and bam!—another hit record." Charting at #14, it was their first Top 20 tune since 1960, and suddenly they were a hot national act once again.

Their very next release was the classic "Washed Ashore." "We were in Chicago performing at the Lamplighter, and Popcorn said, 'I got another hit for you,'" Turner said. "He was thinking in terms of summertime and the beach, and we took the song into the studio and we nailed it. I said, 'Hell yeah! I like this. Another hit.'" And though it didn't make a huge impact on

The Platters. *Courtesy of Sonny Turner.*

the charts, stalling at #56, as one of those "beach music about the beach" songs it has been a fan favorite for decades.

But the group's resurgence was brief, and after a couple of additional chart hits, the group once more faded into the background. It wasn't so much because of the group, however, and Turner thinks it was due more to their management. "Buck Ram had a few hits under his belt, and he thought he was Svengali. I always feel like had Buck stayed out of the way, we might have had four or five more hits, but as it was, that was it." Soon the group splintered again, with Turner himself leaving eventually. He still performs today, however, and says that although the Platters are known for many hits, crowds "even out west, where I've been playing for twenty-five years, expect to hear those songs we did in the mid-'60s—they love those songs." Beach music audiences do too and consider those Musicor tunes the Platters' greatest achievements, no matter what they might have done in the years before.

THE RADIANTS

"IT AIN'T NO BIG THING"
1965, Billboard #91
Chess 1925

It would be hard to find a group that was more fractious and ever-changing than the Radiants. In a ten-year career that produced nearly twenty single recordings, there were never more than two consecutive records that were produced with exactly the same lineup of personnel singing. Based on singles such as "Ain't No Big Thing" and "Voice Your Choice" (almost the only time the group did actually record two consecutive songs with the same lineup), perhaps had they been able to overcome their compatibility issues their history might have been more successful as a group. But that was not to be.

The Radiants got their start as youth choir singers in Chicago. Maurice McCallister not only put the group together but would also serve as one of two constants throughout most of the group's recordings—Wallace Sampson being the other. Other members at the start were Jerome Brooks, Elzie Butler and Charles Washington. They realized their future probably wasn't in gospel recordings, however, and they started trying to edge into the R&B market by 1961. Despite the fact that many labels turned them down, they were persistent, and Chess finally signed them. But even before they had their first recording, they had a personnel change, as Washington was replaced by Green McLauren.

Their first release, the 1962 single "Father Knows Best," did not chart, nor did the subsequent single "Heartbreak Society." On the next release, 1963's "Shy Guy," in another of many personnel changes, Frank McCollum replaced Green McLauren, who had been drafted. From this point on, the lineup changed so often it is nearly impossible to accurately pin it down for more than a one-year period. After recording another failed single as Maurice and the Radiants in 1964, the group broke up. They almost immediately re-formed with just Sampson and McCallister from the previous group, and in 1964, with Leonard Caston Jr., they recorded "Voice Your Choice" as a trio. It went to #51 on the Billboard Top 100 and #16 on the R&B charts. They finally seemed to have found the right combination of talent, and the result was their first chart hit.

Chess also realized this trio had the perfect blend of voices and used them as backup singers on Tony Clarke's "The Entertainer" as well as Billy Stewart's "Sitting in the Park. "The Entertainer" was Chess catalogue #1924, and the Radiants' next single, "It Ain't No Big Thing," was the next record the label released at #1925. The sound on "It Ain't No Big Thing" would seem to have confirmed that they finally found the group lineup that clicked. This mellow, harmonious-sounding record, with McCallister and Caston alternating as lead and Maurice White (later of Earth, Wind and Fire) on drums, gave them another chart success. Though it only went to #91 on the Billboard charts, it actually outperformed "Voice Your Choice" on the R&B charts, getting as high as #14.

Stability, however, was not to be the group's standard. After recording one more record as a trio, in 1965 Caston left the group, and later McCallister left to pursue a solo career and record duets with Green McLauren beginning in 1967 as Maurice and Mac. McCallister's departure should have signaled the end of the group once and for all, but in a move evocative of some of the Drifters' early personnel changes, Chess decided to take "Don't It Make You Feel Kinda Bad," a single recorded by another group that had split up, the Confessions, and release it as a Radiants disc in 1966. The lead singer of that group, Mitchell Bullock, was teamed with Sampson, Jameson and Caston's brother Victor to create a new incarnation of the Radiants. The record did moderately well, and although it didn't make the pop chart, it did go to #47 on the R&B chart. "Hold On" did a little better in 1968, hitting #68 on the pop chart, but that was the end of their chart success, and they left Chess the next year. They broke up for good in 1972.

With their frequent personnel changes, the Radiants stand as a textbook case of a group whose instability probably derailed what could have been a long and productive career. Certainly "It Ain't No Big Thing" would seem to indicate that this could have and should have been the case.

JIMMY RICKS
AND THE RAVENS

"GREEN EYES"
1955, pre-Billboard
Jubilee 5203

The Ravens are the oldest established group discussed in this book, and as a result they have a more thorough discography than almost anyone on the list. They recorded nearly sixty singles before they even recorded "Green Eyes" in 1955, and they would record a few more songs after that as well. However, no song they did in their long and successful career would capture the ears of beach music lovers more than "Green Eyes," and many would echo Linda "Quig" Quinlan James of the Monzas, who told me that "Green Eyes" was one of her favorite beach songs because "it just reminds me of OD and the beach—period."

The Ravens started out in the 1940s as Jimmy Ricks, Warren Suttles, Ollie Jones and Leonard Puzey. The group has been credited with many innovations, including perhaps being the first to use a bird name for a group and being the first to use dance steps in their performances. After a few recordings with Ricks, Jones and Puzey alternating as leads, in 1947 they added tenor Maithe Marshall as yet another lead voice. From that point on, the group really seemed to find its identity, appearing in shows with the Artie Shaw Orchestra, Dinah Washington and Amos Milburn. Tour stops included concerts in Las Vegas and Hawaii and an appearance on Ed Sullivan's *Toast of the Town*. Throughout the period, and despite a plethora of good voices in the group, generally they featured the bass singer Ricks as the frontman.

The Classic Years

In 1950, the Ravens moved to the Columbia label, where their career was overseen by Mitch Miller. Because Miller chose to feature Ricks on their records, sometimes in duets with other acts and occasionally as a single act, this was the beginning of the same type of internal dissension that beset many other successful groups. There had already been several personnel changes over the years, and Puzey and Marshall finally quit the group in 1951 (Suttles had already departed), though Marshall returned after Puzey was drafted.

From that point on, the group went through change after change, and they signed with Jubilee records in 1955. They were a popular act by this point—commanding up to $2,000 a night—and seemed poised for even bigger and better things with Jubilee. Their first song there was "Bye Bye Baby Blues." Their second, "Green Eyes," was a remake of an old Jimmy Dorsey song that today stands as a beach music staple. Ricks's deep bass voice, complemented by Ravens member Jimmy Stewart, made the song their most successful to date. But after just two more singles for Jubilee, Ricks decided to go solo for good. As a group, the Ravens tried to soldier on but were never successful again. On his own, though he recorded for a half dozen labels, Ricks never had a big solo hit, despite the fact that he continued to record into the late 1960s. 1961's "You're the Boss" with LaVern Baker is probably his most notable post-Ravens hit. At the end of his career he was back at Jubilee, cutting his last single for them, "Wigglin' and Gigglin'," in 1968. He then became a vocalist for the Count Basie Orchestra and was still singing in that capacity when he died in 1974.

Like many other vocal groups, the Ravens had a tumultuous history, but at least they stayed together long enough to record a large body of significant work in the '40s and '50s. In their catalogue, "Green Eyes" stands paramount as an acknowledged beach music classic.

DIANA ROSS AND MARVIN GAYE

"MY MISTAKE (WAS TO LOVE YOU)"
1974, Billboard #19
Motown 1269

In retrospect, 1974's Diana Ross and Marvin Gaye collaboration "My Mistake" should have been the biggest of big hits, and it's hard to figure out why the song wasn't bigger. It had the pedigree: the vocalists were two of the most popular singers in the world, the songwriters had written and would write several big hits, including several #1 charting songs, and when you throw in Motown's famous Funk Brothers doing the music, you have a recipe guaranteed to produce a winner. Nevertheless, "My Mistake" only climbed as high as #19, and as a result the record must have been a bit of a disappointment for all involved. In the Carolinas, however, the song is considered a beach music classic.

By 1974, both Diana Ross and Marvin Gaye had been churning out hits for more than a decade. Gaye had been one of the 1960s' biggest solo artists, with a series of singles hits that included "I Heard It Through the Grapevine" (#1), "How Sweet It Is to Be Loved By You" (#6) and "Too Busy Thinking About My Baby" (#4), while Ross had spent most of the 1960s as the lead singer for the Supremes, who had had twelve #1 singles, including "Where Did Our Love Go," "Baby Love" and "Stop! In the Name of Love." By 1970, Ross had gone out on her own, but even as a singles artist, by 1974 she was coming off a string of nine Top 40 singles, including "Ain't No Mountain High Enough"(#1) and "Touch Me in the Morning" (#1). With the coming of the '70s, Gaye's music had become more visionary and socially conscious, so during that period he had produced "What's Going On" (#2), "Mercy Mercy Me" (#4) and "Let's Get It On" (#1). As a result, just thinking about an album with two of Motown's biggest artists with the combined track record of Gaye and Ross, Motown mogul Berry Gordy was no doubt seeing dollar signs.

It wasn't quite as simple as that, however. Reportedly, Gaye had sworn never to record a duet again after the death of his favorite singing partner, Tammi Terrell, in 1970. Apparently Gordy gave him no option about recording with Ross and ordered him to do so. Forced into the partnership, and further resenting what Gaye reportedly saw as the promotion of Ross's career more so than his own, Gaye undoubtedly went into the arrangement feeling a bit bullied. Gaye by this time was also reportedly smoking pot constantly, and when recording began for the album that was to become *Diana and Marvin*, Ross was pregnant and consequently worried that Gaye's smoking in the studio would have an adverse effect on her health and the health of her unborn child. Ross begged Gordy to make Gaye stop the smoking in the studio, Gaye refused and, as a result, the songs were recorded with each artist in a different studio and mixed together and overdubbed later. While this is not apparent on "My Mistake"—the chemistry seems good—the same cannot be said for the whole album that resulted from their collaboration.

The album was released in 1973, and the first single from the album, "You're a Special Part of Me," reached #12 on the charts. The second single, "My Mistake," seemed like it would be a surefire hit. Not only was it written by a team of great songwriters—Gloria Jones (writer of the Four Tops' "Just Seven Numbers" and Gladys Knight and the Pips' "If I Were Your Woman") and Pam Sawyer (cowriter of the Supremes' "Love Child" and later of Ross's #1 hit "Love Hangover")—but with instrumentation by the Funk Brothers, it had it all. With its sweet, meaningful vocals, it *sounds* like Gaye and Ross have the perfect chemistry, despite the real-life friction in the studio. It's a powerful song.

For all that, "My Mistake" only reached #19 on the charts, and two subsequent singles from the album would not do even that well in the U.S. Though the album sold more than one million copies, it only went as high as #25 on the album charts, so in the United States it was viewed as somewhat of a failure—especially given the talent assembled for it. Both artists would go on to have subsequent #1 hits on their own, and as such the *Diana and Marvin* album and "My Mistake" are somewhat of an afterthought on the résumés of both Ross and Gaye in the 1970s. Despite this, "My Mistake" is a genuine beach music shagging classic.

JIMMY RUFFIN

"WHAT BECOMES OF THE BROKENHEARTED"
1966, Billboard #7
Soul 35022

Soul supergroup the Spinners didn't have a big hit until "It's a Shame" went to #14 for them in 1970; one wonders what would have happened had they recorded a song intended for them in 1966, "What Becomes of the Brokenhearted." Instead, Jimmy Ruffin recorded the song and took it to the Top 10, and while the Spinners would have to wait four more years for their first big hit, Ruffin became a Motown superstar almost overnight.

As the son of a minister, Jimmy Ruffin grew up singing gospel music in the church. After a childhood stint with his brother David in the group the Dixie Nightingales, in 1961 he recorded one solo side on Motown's Miracle label, but "Don't Feel Sorry for Me" didn't make any chart noise before Ruffin was drafted. After his enlistment was up, he recorded a few failed sides before receiving an offer to join the Temptations in 1964. Feeling that he was better suited for a solo career, he turned them down but recommended his brother David instead.

As a solo artist for Motown's Soul subsidiary, he recorded a couple of unsuccessful tracks before hearing about a tune William Witherspoon, Paul Riser and James Dean had written for another Motown group, the Spinners. At the time, the Spinners had recorded several songs but had still not had a breakout, as only "I'll Always Love You" had made the Top 40. Nevertheless, Ruffin convinced the powers at Motown to let him have the song, and thus it was Ruffin, and not the Spinners, who recorded "What Becomes of the Brokenhearted" in 1966.

The song seemed to appeal to anyone who had ever loved and lost before. Interestingly, the song originally had a spoken introduction, where Ruffin said,

A world filled with love is a wonderful sight.
Being in love is one's heart's delight.
But that look of love isn't on my face.
That enchanted feeling has been replaced.

This version was about twelve seconds longer and, after the intro, rolled right into Ruffin singing "As I walk this land, of broken dreams…" However, the decision was made to remove the intro and begin the song with the powerful Funk Brothers instrumentals, which now seems an indispensable part of the song. Listeners certainly liked it as released; it went to #7 in the Top 40 and #6 on the R&B charts. It went to number #10 in the UK, and like many quality songs rereleased during the Northern Soul explosion in England, it charted even higher the second time around, reaching #4 in 1974.

Ruffin's next release was the fine "I've Passed This Way Before" (1966), which went to #17, followed by 1967's "Gonna Give Her All the Love I've Got"(#29) and "Don't You Miss Me a Little Bit" (#68). Though each American release was less successful than the previous one, in England, his records were doing increasingly better. While "I'll Say Forever My Love" (1968) only reached #77 in the U.S., it went to #7 in the UK. "I've Passed This Way Before" was reissued in England in 1969 and went to #33, and "Farewell Is a Lonely Sound" (1969) went to #8 in the UK even though it didn't chart at all in the States. Even his last big hit, 1980's "Hold On to My Love," would chart higher in England (#7) than in the U.S. (#10). By the 1980s, Ruffin had actually moved to England, where his work was clearly much more popular and where his music continued to chart well into the '80s.

"What Becomes of the Brokenhearted" would go on to be recorded by many groups, and Robson & Jerome would later take their version of the song to #1 in the UK. The Isley Brothers also did a version in the 1960s called "Smile," with different words set to the exact same backing tracks. As for the Spinners, the group that was supposed to record the song, their highest charting record for Motown would be 1970's "It's a Shame," though after they left for Atlantic they found immeasurable success. But for millions of listeners the world over, and especially for beach music lovers, it's Ruffin's recording of "What Becomes of the Brokenhearted" that stands as the greatest version and a bona fide beach music classic.

THE SHOWMEN

"IT WILL STAND"
1961, Billboard #61
Minit 632

"39-21-40 SHAPE"
1963, did not chart
Minit 662

Of the wide variety of singers and acts found on this survey, General Norman Johnson was the lead singer on more of the Top 100 songs—five all told—than any other artist. That he did this with two different groups, the Showmen and the Chairmen of the Board, is amazing, and perhaps that's why Johnson's gravelly voice and unparalleled showmanship make most people consider him in many ways the most recognizable figure in the beach music world. Considering that four of the five records were also national hits, Johnson can truly lay claim to being one of the most influential individuals in beach music.

The Showmen were a Virginia-based group who began as the Humdingers in the early 1950s. The group, consisting of General Norman Johnson (his given name), Milton Wells, Gene Knight, Dorsey Knight and Leslie Felton, recorded a few unreleased early sides for Atlantic in 1956, but when they took on manager Noah Biggs, he had the ambition to make the group more than just a competent local act. He had the group record a few demos and sent these to New Orleans–based producer Joe Banashak. After insisting that the group change their name, the newly christened Showmen recorded a number of sides on the Minit label with an up-and-coming talent in the recording industry named Allan Toussaint. Minit artists included Ernie K. Doe, Irma Thomas and Benny Spellman, so the Showmen were squarely in the middle of the burgeoning New Orleans R&B scene of the early 1960s. (In fact, K. Doe's "Mother-in-Law" would be released just before the Showmen's first single, and Spellman's "Lipstick Traces" would be released just afterward.)

The first of the Showmen's records released was "Country Fool" on Minit 362, but it was the record's flip side, "It Will Stand" (originally written with the title "Rock and Roll Will Stand"), that got the bulk of the airplay and charted. The homage to rock-and-roll went to #61 on the Hot 100 and #40 on the R&B charts. Considering how this song has become such an anthem for beach music *and* rock-and-roll, in retrospect it wasn't a very significant showing. Nevertheless, as their first chart record and first record for Minit, it was a promising start.

Their next three Minit releases in 1961 and 1962 would all fail to find an audience, as would their fifth Minit release, the now classic "39-21-40 Shape." Johnson told writer Jim Newsom in 2007, "I was only about 14 years old when I wrote that song," and he didn't actually know any girl with a 39-21-40 shape. "I don't know," Johnson said, "maybe it rhymed with 'ape-itty ape.' That came from a young teenager's brain!" But the exact title depends on who you listen to and what you read. Minit released the single with the much more provocative measurements "39-21-46" on the label, and Johnson stated that though Minit claimed it was a clerical and printing error, he didn't believe it. He told Newsom, "I think they did it as a ploy because it was more commercial, it aroused curiosity." As a result, though the label says "39-21-46," the lyrics of course always say "39-21-40 Shape." Even if listeners were curious, however, they didn't buy the record, and it failed to chart.

A failure to sustain any chart success soon led to the group and the label parting ways, and most of the Minit recordings were eventually purchased by Imperial. Perhaps feeling that "It Will Stand" had the potential to do better than its first release indicated, Imperial rereleased the song in 1964, and this time it rose as high as #80 during its three weeks on the chart. Other Imperial efforts by the Showmen failed to chart, however, so after a period of inactivity, eventually the group moved to Swan. There they would record several sides, including "Our Love Will Grow" in 1965, which would track at #382 on Kev Roberts's list of the Northern Soul all-time Top 500 songs. The group continued to record singles periodically before Johnson decided to form a new group, the Chairmen of the Board, in 1968. The Showmen continued recording with Felton on lead vocals but would never again have a chart hit.

Of course General Johnson, as we now know, was just getting started. The Showmen, however, left a legacy of great music and two beach classics in "It Will Stand" and "39-21-40 Shape."

BENNY SPELLMAN

"LIPSTICK TRACES"
1962, Billboard #80
Minit 644

T he story behind 'Lipstick Traces' is that because Benny believed his bass
voice was so instrumental in making 'Mother-in-Law' a hit, he worried
Allen Toussaint to death to write him a song that sounded similar to it,"
Deacon John Moore told me in an interview. Moore, who played on "Mother-
in-Law" as well as "Lipstick Traces," noted that Benny "kept hounding Allen
and hounding him. 'Please write me a song,' Benny would say. He wanted
a song that would work with his bass vocals." Though most would think
Spellman would have felt good about the fact that he'd been able to sing on
one of the all-time great #1 singles in "Mother-in-Law," he wanted a hit song
all his own. "So, Allen did write him his own song—'Lipstick Traces,'" Moore
said. And though it didn't chart as well as "Mother-in-Law," "Lipstick Traces"
is just as big, if not bigger, on the list of all-time greatest beach music hits.

Unlike many of the artists in this book who seemed to have settled on
singing as a career from an early age, Benny Spellman apparently had no such
ideas. If anything, he seemed to back into the singing opportunities that came
along. As a college student on a football scholarship at Southern University,
Spellman joined a local singing group, but that ended with his induction into
the army. After his discharge, he returned to his hometown of Pensacola,
Florida, and there he ran into Huey "Piano" Smith and his group the Clowns
in 1959. Smith eventually invited Spellman to join the Clowns, and Spellman
performed with that group and then later went out on his own after positive
reactions at an impromptu live performance in New Orleans. A lot of people

liked what they were hearing, and Spellman was signed to Minit records. His first records for Minit, "Life Is Too Short" and "Darling No Matter Where," both recorded in 1960, failed to generate any substantial sales.

Minit had another recording artist, Ernie K. Doe, who was struggling to find his sound as well, and one day Spellman agreed to help out on one of Doe's recordings as a background singer. The song was "Mother-in-Law," which skyrocketed up the charts to #1. Spellman's bass voice can be heard echoing Doe by singing the words "mother-in-law" throughout the record, so oddly enough his first brush with chart success was for another artist. But Spellman would soon find success with his own record "Lipstick Traces," which climbed to #80 in June 1962. Deacon John Moore told me he felt like it just had to be a hit, because "if you listen, 'Lipstick Traces' is almost identical to 'Mother-in-Law,' with the same chord changes but a different story line. If you listen to the melodic line, 'Don't leave me no more,' it's the same as 'Mother-in-law.' He used that little hook to construct 'Lipstick Traces' because Allen said Benny bugged him so much he just sat down to write a song like 'Mother-in-Law.' Allen was able to write around people's personalities and vocal styles, and he successfully did it with Benny and K. Doe. And though the songs, construction-wise, were similar, they had their own identity because of the personalities of the different singers. Benny was a baritone bass, and K. Doe was a tenor. So Allen knew how to write for both of them and yet give them individuality at the same time."

The flip side, "Fortune Teller," was a minor hit in its own right, and it was later recorded by the Rolling Stones, the Hollies and the Who, among others. "In New Orleans, 'Fortune Teller' was more popular than 'Lipstick Traces,'" Moore said, "because it had that Latin rhythm to it, and it was a huge song, with that bass line that was Benny's trademark." It was also apparently the key to Spellman's popular live performances. "He had a stage show that was unbelievable. The audience would sing along with him. He'd do all these crazy antics, pull off his coat and throw it out in the audience. And because he was an ex-football player, he'd roll up his shirtsleeves and show them his muscles. He'd get down in the crowd, put a rag around his head and dance like a fortuneteller, like a swami. He had the whole audience eating out of the palm of his hand. He was a fabulous entertainer."

Despite the fact that other groups would record his work, Spellman himself would have no more chart success and would retire from the music business in 1968; a brief comeback in the 1980s would be cut short by a stroke. But as the mournful voice on his own classic "Lipstick Traces" and the backup on "Mother-in-Law," beach music fans would say he had more than enough success, even if not the chart kind.

THE SPINNERS

"IT'S A SHAME"
1970, Billboard #14
VIP 25057

After I signed with Motown and joined the group, Stevie Wonder and I became very good friends," Spinners lead singer G.C. Cameron told me. "We'd hang out together, and he knew that because I'd been thrown in the midst of all these great Motown singers like Marvin Gaye, David Ruffin, Levi Stubbs and Diana Ross, I needed to catch up. So one night we were out and he told me, 'I wrote a song for you.' I asked him what it was, and he had me take him to his house and he started playing this song on his electric piano. The song was 'It's a Shame.'" And while for the casual listener the Spinners' story begins about 1972 when they kicked off a long string of hits on Atlantic records that would include "I'll Be Around," "Could It Be I'm Falling in Love" and "One of a Kind (Love Affair)," in reality, they had by that time been recording for almost a decade in near anonymity on Motown. "It's a Shame" was their first Top 20 song and a portent of the mainstream popularity that was yet to come.

The Spinners had some early success on the pop charts in 1961 on the Tri-Phi label, including "That's What Girls Are Made For" (#27). In 1963, Berry Gordy bought out Tri-Phi, so by 1964 the Spinners were part of Motown's considerable array of talent. Despite the fact that they had a couple of brushes with chart success, including 1965's "I'll Always Love You" (#35) and 1966's "Truly Yours" (#111), they were largely underutilized at Motown and frequently even served as chaperones and chauffeurs for other Motown acts. Cameron, who joined the group to replace former lead Chico Edwards in 1967, told me, "Yes, a lot of the guys were working doing odd jobs for different acts at Motown. I was fortunate that I never had to do it, but some of the other guys in the group would sometimes go and cart other artists back and forth and drive the limo. But you know, it was making a living—that's what it was—it was surviving." Eventually the Spinners were relegated to the Motown subsidiary label VIP, and given the recognition factor this name conjures compared to the other Gordy-owned labels such as Motown and Tamla, it would appear that the group was essentially being sent down to the minors to play out the remainder of their contract.

That's when the group's big break came. After Wonder played the song for Cameron that night, "the next day Stevie went in and recorded the track and three or four days later I went into the studio with the rest of the Spinners to record the vocal track." Cameron sang "both leads" on the song, and he explained, "that means that I not only sang the part when it says 'It's a shame, the way you mess around with your man,' but the higher chorus when it says 'why do you use me, try to confuse me' and so on. We did the song in one take, and Stevie and everyone else was really excited. That's how 'It's a Shame' came about."

But even Cameron was unprepared for the song's success. "I didn't think much of anything about 'It's a Shame' being special when it came out," he said. "There was too much music, too many hits. I felt like anything coming out of Motown had the chance to be a hit, but I wasn't paying any particular attention to it. I just hoped at the time that we would have the opportunity to have a hit record like so many of the great acts at Motown." "It's a Shame" was that hit, and as it raced to #14 it not only indicated the Spinners' potential, but as the first song Wonder produced for another group, it was an indication of his marketability as more than just a singer as well.

As we now know, "It's a Shame" was just the beginning for the group. After finishing their contract at Motown, the Spinners signed with Atlantic, where they notched twenty-seven subsequent Top 100 hits. But over the course of a long and storied career that even found him living in Myrtle Beach for a while and singing lead on the Tams' "Walkin' Dr. Bill" in 2000, Cameron has come to see that "It's a Shame" is a special song. "Today they won't let me perform anywhere unless I sing that song, and I feel blessed to have it. It never gets old, it never sounds tired—it always sounds like the day we recorded it. Whenever you hear it on the radio it sounds like it's a new record. It's one of a kind."

THE SPIRAL STARECASE

"MORE TODAY THAN YESTERDAY"
1969, Billboard #12
Columbia 44741

I'd had the title 'More Today than Yesterday' for a couple of years before I ever wrote the song," lead vocalist Pat Upton told the author. When he finally did write it, he created one of those big, brassy hits that became the vogue in the late 1960s, and no one did that sound better than the Spiral Starecase. As an example of what is often called "horn rock," the in-your-face sound and up-tempo beat mean that this song sounds a lot different from most beach music classics that are more firmly grounded in rhythm and blues. Nevertheless, the song that evolved from just a title has long been a favorite of beach music fans everywhere.

The group started as a Sacramento combo known as the Fydallions, and they soon evolved into a five-piece group consisting of Harvey Kaye, Dick Lopes, Bobby Raymond, Vinnie Parello and lead vocalist Pat Upton. After playing the club circuit and cutting a few regional discs on the Crusader label, in 1967 they signed with Columbia Records. But while Columbia loved their sound, they hated their conservative clothes and hairstyles, as well as the name of the group. The group's appearance was made over, and their name was changed to the Spiral Starecase, being deliberately misspelled so as to not too closely imitate its source, the movie *The Spiral Staircase*.

Their first record, "Baby What I Mean," didn't go anywhere, and so "when we were in Las Vegas in '68, Columbia suggested that someone in the group should write our songs, so I was the one," Upton told me. "I already

The Spiral Starecase.
Courtesy of Candy Kaye.

had the title, and when I was jamming with a friend he showed me a passing chord that I loved. I knew I would never use that chord with the stuff we were doing and decided the only way was to write a song and use it, and I did. When the chorus came around those words 'I Love You More Today than Yesterday' just fell right into place." Candy Kaye, widow of band member Harvey Kaye, told the author that her husband liked to tell people how they soon knew they had a hit. "We were staying at the Bali Hai Motel in Las Vegas where we were performing as the house band in the Flamingo Sky Room. To test it out, we would play the song just to see if people would dance to it. Every time we played it, people would ask who originally did the song and where could they get it, so we knew we had a hit on our hands." Indeed they did have a hit; it went to #12 on the charts and would eventually sell more than one million copies and earn the group a gold record.

The future looked bright; the group toured with Three Dog Night, Creedence Clearwater Revival, Sly and the Family Stone and the Beach Boys and did *American Bandstand*. They cut an album to showcase "More Today than Yesterday" and, hopefully, a few more hit singles. Unfortunately, the follow-ups to "More," while doing well, did not match the success of

The Spiral Starecase. *Courtesy of Candy Kaye.*

their predecessor. "No One for Me to Turn To" peaked at #52 in 1969, and the superb "She's Ready" reached #72 in 1970. In the meantime, apparently the band members, management and the label were squabbling over money that wasn't being paid out properly, and so just eighteen months after climbing the charts and earning a gold record, "She's Ready" would be their last single and the group would disband in 1971. Upton became a session musician and most notably worked with Ricky Nelson. Kaye put together a new lineup and kept the band's name alive by touring for many years afterward.

"I'm familiar with beach music and have performed in the Carolinas a number of times over the years," Upton said. "I really consider it an honor that our music is recognized as such." "More Today than Yesterday" clearly is recognized as a great beach music classic.

BILLY STEWART

"FAT BOY"
1962, did not chart
Chess 1820

"I DO LOVE YOU"
1965, Billboard #26
Chess 1922

"SITTING IN THE PARK"
1965, Billboard #24
Chess 1932

It's hard to predict what might have happened with Billy Stewart's career had he not died in a car crash at the very young age of thirty-two. He had been successful throughout the 1960s, but by 1970 his career seemed to have lost momentum. While we will never know if he would have found himself in the spotlight once again, he did leave behind three classic beach tunes in "I Do Love You," "Fat Boy" and "Sitting in the Park."

Stewart was involved in music at an early age as a member of his family's group, the Stewart Gospel Singers, and later in the Four Stewart Brothers. Billy won a talent show singing the George Gershwin tune "Summertime" when he was a teenager, but his first real break came when Bo Diddley heard his piano playing skills and asked him to join his band. Stewart became more diversified as he learned to play a variety of instruments, including the bass and the drums, and he recorded his first song, "Billy's

Blues," with Diddley on guitar, on Chess in 1956. Though the record met with some success, it wasn't a national hit, nor were subsequent singles, and Stewart would spend the next five years as a background singer and player and not as a featured act.

But Chess hired a new A&R man, Roquel Davis, and he encouraged Stewart to record once again. His first recording was 1962's "Reap What You Sow," which went to #18 on the R&B charts and #79 on the Billboard Hot 100. During the session, he enlisted the services of his cousin Grace Ruffin and her group the Four Jewels, who within a short time would change their name to simply the Jewels and have their own hit "Opportunity," which also has an entry in this book. Perhaps more importantly, the flip side of the record was a song Davis had asked Stewart to write and record based on his nickname, "Fat Boy." Though "Fat Boy" did not chart, it got a fair amount of airplay and would become Stewart's signature song.

Stewart had a couple of other releases before his next single, "Strange Feeling," went to #25 on the R&B chart and #70 on the pop chart in 1963. He had his first really big hit in 1965 with "I Do Love You," which went to #6 on the R&B charts and #26 on the Top 40. With his brother Johnny on the backing vocals, the record stayed on the charts for twenty-one weeks, and suddenly Stewart was a hot commodity. His very next release was another hit that same year, "Sitting in the Park," which did even better than "I Do Love You," going to #4 on the R&B charts and #24 on the Top 40. That record featured the backing vocals of another Chess act, the Radiants, who

had charted with "Voice Your Choice" in 1964 and had just recorded "It Ain't No Big Thing" in 1965.

Stewart would release several more records before he would go back to his roots and sing that old standard "Summertime" again. Davis had in fact convinced him to do a whole album of standards, and it was a good call. "Summertime" would go to #7 on the R&B charts and #10 in the Top 40, and his next release, his 1967

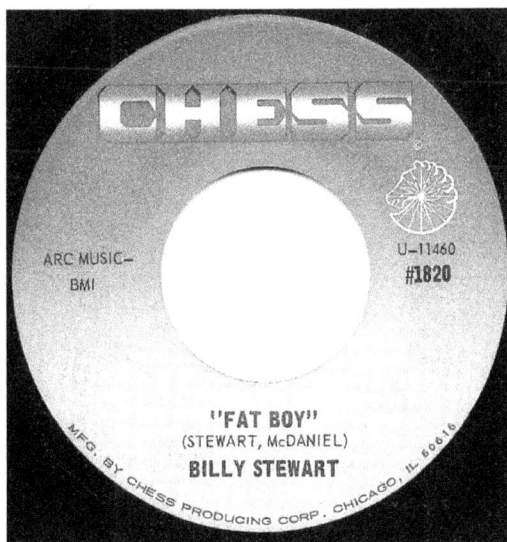

161

version of Doris Day's classic "Secret Love," would go to #11 on the R&B charts and #29 on the pop charts.

After 1967, the Top 40 hits quit coming, and it appeared that Stewart's days as a viable chart presence may have ended. But by this time he was having more serious issues than just failing to have a chart record. His weight was causing increasing problems, he developed diabetes and in 1969, he had a motorcycle accident. Tragically, less than a year later, he was killed while on tour when the car he and three band members were in plunged off a bridge and into the Neuse River near Smithfield, North Carolina. He was just short of thirty-three years old.

There's no telling what Stewart's career might have done had he lived longer. Perhaps he would have become a viable recording artist again, or he may have ended his career playing oldies shows or in some other capacity in the music business. Despite his relatively short life, he nevertheless produced three fantastic beach music classics that thrill audiences even today.

SUNNY AND PHYLLIS

"IF WE HAD TO DO IT ALL OVER"
1968, did not chart
Uni 55091

If We Had to Do It All Over' was a good shag record," Sonny Threatt said in an interview for this book. "Guerry Sample told me it stayed on the jukebox at the Pad at OD for over twenty years and on the jukebox at the Tally Ho in Columbia (which he owned) for longer than that. It was played in both places until it literally wore out." And no wonder: Sunny and Phyllis was one of the lucky few regional groups to record with a national label, and their song was a beach music jukebox perennial as well.

Sonny Threatt's first group was the Greenville High–based Swinging Tangents, but it was his second group, the Nomads, that gave him his first real taste of the big time. That group cut a few sides, and their second release on Mo-Groove records, "Somethin's Bad," is highly collectible and a popular tune on the English Northern Soul scene. Before long, the group's lineup changed, and Threatt, Darrel McClinton and Hugh Martin were joined by Andy Mckinney, Carrol Cox and Phyllis Brown (who was co-lead singer), and Sunny and Phyllis and the Nomads were born. They landed a national recording contract at Los Angeles–based Uni records, and things were starting to click.

Before their first Uni national release, the label insisted on a few changes. First, they wanted to change the backup band's name from the Nomads ("it was a far too common name for bands nationwide"), and since "Uni had the copyright on the name Danes, we agreed to change the band's name to

Sunny and Phyllis. *Courtesy of Sonny Threatt.*

that," Threatt said. Also, Sonny's name was changed to "Sunny" at Uni's request to avoid confusion because "Sonny and Cher had split up" that year and apparently Uni feared audiences might think Sonny was Sonny Bono, re-teamed with another female co-lead—which could get complicated.

So with their new names in place, Sunny and Phyllis and the Danes released "I've Been Lost," and although it didn't make any national noise, Threatt remembered that it was big on the Carolina coast and was "#1 at WTGR AM Myrtle Beach six weeks in a row that summer." Their next release was the now classic "If We Had to Do It All Over." Despite its status as a seminal beach song, nationally it didn't make much noise, failing to break the Top 100. Yet while many groups discussed in this book were allowed multiple chances to break into the Top 100 by their labels, after allowing Sunny and Phyllis to cut just two singles, Uni severed ties with the group. Threatt felt like the re-emergence and regrouping of Sonny and Cher on television and in Vegas made the confusion over the group's identity a liability; "the Sonny and Cher return that summer to the Smothers Brothers summer show killed us as far as Uni was concerned."

Sunny and Phyllis recorded over a dozen more records over the next few years on small labels, "but eventually the band dispersed, most of us going back to school. We had always worked the music in between school, playing live mainly in summers and weekends." Sonny Threatt and Phyllis Brown got married, and though they settled down and did work in advertising, "we really never stopped the music. I guess nobody who's been in it ever does. Back then the larger radio stations (like WTOB Winston Salem or WTGR Myrtle Beach) would have promotion shows once a year or so. They would bring in six or eight acts to a stadium or auditorium and each of us would do our record and maybe one more song. Phyllis and I would come out and sing our records with the stage bands for a while. It was great money, but the sound was not as good as having your own band. I do miss those shows though because the audiences were great and it was fun to meet other entertainers from all over the country."

"Looking back on it," Sonny Threatt says, "we would have gotten more airplay if we had started out with another name. Using our real names was a mistake and being linked with Sonny and Cher was not an asset to our career at all." Despite the fact that today "we've never wanted to do oldies shows—we've always thought that would spoil a great memory," beach music lovers will always have those worn-out 45s—like the ones that played on the jukeboxes at the Pad and the Tally Ho—to listen to and remember.

THE SWINGIN' MEDALLIONS

"DOUBLE SHOT (OF MY BABY'S LOVE)"
1966, Billboard #17
Smash 2033

Probably the most famous statement ever written about beach music comes from the pen of southern writer Lewis Grizzard, who in 1993 wrote: "Even today, when I hear the Swingin' Medallions sing 'Double Shot of My Baby's Love,' it makes me want to stand outside in the hot sun with a milkshake cup full of beer in one hand and a slightly drenched nineteen-year-old coed in the other." That may be the greatest compliment a band can get, and it pretty much epitomizes beach music—good music and good times. And, as Grizzard noted, absolutely nothing says good music and good times like the Swingin' Medallions singing "Double Shot (of My Baby's Love)."

The Medallions got together in 1962 at Lander College in Greenwood, South Carolina. Group founder John McElrath and his friends formed the band to make a little extra money to help pay for school. Their act was based in rhythm and blues, and like many local bands during the '60s, they made their living lining up gigs to play across the South. After a few years in the clubs and on the campus party circuit, McElrath and the group—now consisting of Carroll Bledsoe, Steve Caldwell, Jim Doares, Brent Forston, Charlie Webber, Jimmy Perkins and Joe Morris—wanted to record "Double Shot," a huge regional hit that had been originally recorded by Dick Holler and the Holidays. "I had heard it played in Columbia at USC in the 1950s,"

The Swingin' Medallions. *Courtesy of John McElrath.*

McElrath told me. "It was a local hit when I was a teenager, and when we put our band together we started to play it too."

Eventually, the group was encouraged to record the song. "We were with Bill Lowery in Atlanta, and they kept trying to have us record it with different arrangements and in different ways with horns and so forth that didn't fit the song. We wanted to play it live like we did at shows, so we just took off and went to Arthur Smith Studios in Charlotte. We actually pulled in people off the street and had a big crowd in the studio to make background noise, and that party atmosphere gave us the sound we were looking for." With that version, everything clicked. Initially the record was released on their For Sale label, and they sold them at their performances, but the record got some airplay and really started to take off. Soon they added the "Swingin'" moniker to the Medallions name, and history was made.

Smash records liked what they heard, but before distributing the record nationally they wanted the song altered a bit. McElrath said, "They didn't like some lines, like 'Woke up this morning, my head hurt so bad/ The worst hangover that I ever had,' and made us change it to 'worst morning after that I ever had'—which was stupid, I thought." But even with the changes it worked, and the single was released and became a million-seller, going all the way to #17 on the charts. "It was strange, really, because it had moved up on the charts before it got played up North and out West and became a hit. It helped us as far as our touring went because it was so popular."

The group next released "She Drives Me Out of My Mind," another great beach tune. "Freddie Weller, a friend of ours with Bill Lowery, wrote the song. They wanted it to be as close to 'Double Shot' as we could make it." Despite—or maybe because of—the similarities, the record stalled at #71, and their next release was another party track, a version of Bruce Channel's "Hey! Baby" called "Hey, Hey Baby." It did not chart but has become a southern party staple nonetheless.

Eventually, band members went their separate ways, most going back to college to finish their educations. While McElrath is now the only original band member still with the group, the Swingin' Medallions still continue to wow crowds as they have for nearly fifty years. "We had a lot of fun," he said. "I think we just lucked into it." Luck or not, the song and the band have become legends. Fittingly, perhaps Grizzard put it best: "I have asked often what, if anything, endures? Well, the Swingin' Medallions and their kind of music—my generation's music—has." Beach music lovers would certainly agree.

THE TAMS

"WHAT KIND OF FOOL (DO YOU THINK I AM?)"
1963, Billboard #9
ABC-Paramount 10502

"I'VE BEEN HURT"
1965, did not chart
ABC-Paramount 10741

"BE YOUNG, BE FOOLISH, BE HAPPY"
1968, Billboard #61
ABC 11066

"We recorded so many great songs, and they've kept us working for fifty-one years," Charles Pope said when I asked him to name his favorite Tams' songs. That was exactly the problem when trying to prepare this chapter; when putting together a list of the greatest beach music hits, with most groups' songs it's simply a question of whether to include them or not. With the Tams, the problem is which songs have to be left off the list. Obviously, many great Tams songs are worthy of inclusion, but ultimately, it came down to three Tams classics: "What Kind of Fool (Do You Think I Am?)," "I've Been Hurt" and "Be Young, Be Foolish, Be Happy." As these songs illustrate, the Tams' mix of both southern regionality and national and international success epitomizes beach music and its sometimes even universal appeal.

The Tams consisted of brothers Joe and Charles Pope, Floyd Ashton, Robert Lee Smith and Horace Key, and the group took their name from

The Tams. *Courtesy of Diane Pope.*

their trademark Tam-O-Shanter hats, which was about all in the way of costumes they could afford. Working with Atlanta song publisher and entrepreneur Bill Lowery, in 1962 the group recorded "Untie Me" for Arlen records. That song, written by Joe South, also featured the contributions of Ray Stevens on piano. The song climbed to #62 on the Hot 100 and #12 on the R&B charts, and as a result soon ABC-Paramount picked up their contract and gave their music an even broader national release. Their first ABC recording was "What Kind of Fool (Do You Think I Am?)," but Charles Pope says that he "was surprised by 'What Kind of Fool,'" because he wasn't wild about it and "didn't even want that song to be our second release." Audiences obviously liked it though, and it raced to #9 on the Billboard charts. Both sides of their next record charted, with 1964's "You

The Tams. *Courtesy of Diane Pope.*

Lied to Your Daddy" coming in at #70 and "It's All Right (You're Just In Love)" charting at #79. Their next single, "Hey Girl Don't Bother Me," stalled just outside the Top 40 at #41, and their next song, "Silly Little Girl," another well-loved beach favorite, charted at #87. While the Tams' records weren't always charting high on the pop charts, they were selling records, and the group was developing a huge following.

By this time, Floyd Ashton was replaced with Albert Cottle, but the group continued to turn out the hits, and they were about to begin the most remarkable period of their careers. After several more singles, in 1965 they released "I've Been Hurt," another classic. Though "I've Been Hurt" would not make the pop charts, Pope says it was "a favorite with the college kids," so it became a monster regional hit and was reportedly the best-selling and most often played Tams song of all time—despite the fact that it never made the Hot 100. In 1968, they released the anthemic "Be Young, Be Foolish, Be Happy," which to many beach music lovers epitomizes the beach music experience. "Be Young" was written by Georgia songwriter Ray Whitley, who had written many of the Tams' biggest hits and best-known songs, including "What Kind of Fool," "Laugh It Off," "I've Been Hurt," "Hey Girl, Don't Bother Me" and others. "Be Young" was different, however; "Bill Lowery chose all the songs for us, except for 'Be Young, Be Foolish.' It had been recorded by some other groups, who hadn't had a hit with it, but Joe wanted to do the song, so Bill let us do it," Pope says. While "Be Young" would only hit #61 on the pop charts, it would go to #26 on the R&B charts and would eventually sell more than one million copies and be their only RIAA-Certified Gold Record. Obviously, Joe Pope had an uncanny ability to pick a winner.

Any one of those accolades would put the Tams in their own special category among beach music performers, but as their career was apparently winding down, the Tams still had a few surprises in store for their fans. They released a few more singles, including 1970's special "Tams Medley" on Capitol. In 1971, 1964's "Hey Girl Don't Bother Me" was rereleased in England, went all the way to #1 and was song of the year in the UK. Pope noted that this was a pleasant surprise, and a highlight of the song's popularity was that "we went over and performed at Top of the Pops with Rod Stewart in 1971."

The Tams, it seems, could never be counted out, and in fact their records continued to chart in England well into the late 1980s. The Tams still actively perform and record, even surviving the death of key group member Joe Pope. And while some people would consider any group with just one Top 40 hit on the Billboard Pop Charts a one-hit wonder, the Tams have been anything but that, standing tall as one of the most successful acts in the annals of beach music history. The songs "have kept us working for more than five decades," Pope noted, "and we still work one hundred days a year after all these years. My son Little Redd started with me and my brother Joe when he was seven years old, and he'll be taking over the Tams. That's why I say the Tams will never die." After fifty successful years, odds are he's correct.

WILLIE TEE

"Teasin' You" b/w
"Walking Up a One-Way Street"
1965, Billboard #97
Atlantic 2273

"Thank You John"
1965, did not chart
Atlantic 2287

As far as I'm concerned," said Sonny Threatt of Sunny and Phyllis fame, "my all-time favorite beach record is 'Thank You John.' When you hear 'Thank You John' you've heard the essence of beach music." Many people would probably echo those sentiments about the perennial favorite as well, and those same people would probably be quite surprised to learn that despite the song's pervasive popularity, the song didn't make a dent in the pop charts in 1965 when it was originally released. The same goes for "Walking Up a One-Way Street," but despite their failure to make much noise nationally, both songs and "Teasin' You" are all-time beach music classics.

Willie Tee was born in New Orleans as Wilson Turbinton, where he was surrounded and influenced by the vibrant New Orleans music scene. As he went along picking up local gigs and learning about the business, one person from whom he learned a great deal was his music teacher, Harold Batiste, who had already successfully arranged Sam Cooke's "You Send Me" in 1957 and would also be successful as a producer and arranger on songs such as Barbara George's "I Know," Joe Jones's "You Talk Too Much," Lee

Dorsey's "Ya Ya" and others. He added Wilson to his jazz group, the All for One band, and an associated record label also carried the AFO name. It was for AFO that Wilson—recording for the first time as Willie Tee—recorded his first two singles, and he next recorded on the Cinderella label in 1963. None of the songs was a hit.

However, he really started to find his audience when his cousin Julius Gaines founded New Orleans–based Nola records. The label's eighth single release was "Teasin' You," a song that apparently Tee was reluctant to record because he felt it was too great a departure from the jazz-like sound he was seeking to be known for. But the song quickly found an audience, and after the Righteous Brothers sang "Teasin' You" on the popular music showcase program *Shindig!*, suddenly Tee was a hot property. Atlantic picked up the rights to distribute the song nationally, and it just barely charted at #97. Almost unnoticed was the flip side of the record, the now popular "Walking Up a One-Way Street." That song, in which Tee laments being left alone and almost tortured by his lover, puts into perspective the one-sidedness of their relationship. Plaintive and soulful, Tee's song, though it did not chart, nevertheless touched a nerve with beach music lovers and has remained a classic since its release. Like many beach music songs, its failure to make the national charts has not been an impediment.

The top 100 Billboard slot "Teasin' You" earned was apparently encouraging enough that Atlantic gave Tee another shot, and his next recording for the label was 1965's immortal "Thank You John," which is nowhere near as heart-wrenching as "Walking" and really can't be considered heart-wrenching at all. "Thank You John" is an odd song, or at least the subject matter is. It seems to be about deception, infidelity, physical abuse, pimping, lying—any and all of the above. Lines like "I know he wanted to handle you, I could tell by the bruises on your arm," "If he tries this again/He's gotta shed some blood" and "It's alright to keep her out all night long/but when she leaves you alone/send your paycheck home" tell a story very different from the good times, love and romance themes that make up most popular songs. Perhaps listeners felt like this too, as "Thank You John" failed to connect with fans nationally. Despite the fact that these aren't the things most beach music songs deal with either, nevertheless fans in the Southeast made the song a beach music staple in a very short time indeed.

After "Thank You John" and his next single both failed to chart, Atlantic didn't renew Tee's contract. His next single for Nola was 1966's great "Please Don't Go," now regarded as a pretty good beach tune in its own right. Of his subsequent singles, none really did much outside of the New Orleans area, although a contract with Capitol in 1970 did produce a fine cover of Burt Bacharach and Hal David's "Reach Out for Me." Thereafter, Tee became a mainstay of the New Orleans music scene, performing, producing and recording a variety of music until his death from cancer in 2007.

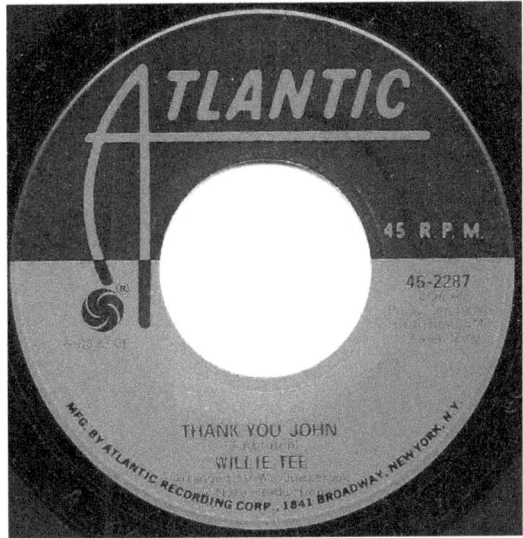

Unlike a lot of other New Orleans–based musicians who were able to turn their Crescent City popularity into a following on a national scale, Willie Tee was never able to make a big impact nationally. In beach music circles, however, Willie Tee's records have come to be regarded, as Sonny Threatt said, as "the essence of beach music."

THE TEMPTATIONS

"MY GIRL"
1965, Billboard #1
Gordy 7038

Considering that books have been written and movies have been made about the Temptations' history, attempting to present an in-depth and comprehensive history of the group here would be a bit superfluous. Their story is fairly well known, and they are by far one of the most important groups in all of popular music during the last fifty years. Above all, however, their single "My Girl" stands not only as one of the greatest songs ever but also as one of beach music's greatest classics.

The original Temptations were formed as the Elgins in 1960 and consisted of Otis Williams, Eldridge Bryant, Melvin Franklin, Eddie Kendricks and Paul Williams. When they signed with Motown, they changed their name to the Temptations, and though they released seven singles in the early '60s, nothing made the Top 40 on the pop charts. The group tried various leads during this period but remained unsuccessful, and it was only when Eldridge Bryant left and David Ruffin (brother of Jimmy Ruffin) joined the group that things started to gel. In 1964, they made some progress toward stardom with "The Way You Do the Things You Do," which featured Kendricks on lead and was their first Top 20 hit. However, it was Ruffin's strong, gravelly, distinctive voice on his first lead performance that brought the group their first #1 hit, the unforgettable "My Girl."

Smokey Robinson had written the song about his wife, Claudette, and as an answer to Mary Wells's hit the previous year "My Guy"—a song

Robinson had also written. Robinson felt it would be perfect for Ruffin's vocal abilities, so he let the Temptations have it instead of giving it to his own group. With the Funk Brothers backing the group and the strong bass line, the song was a hit. The elegant orchestration of the background music also gives the song an airy, romantic feel and made it one of the all-time great classic love songs. The song has remained so popular that artists as diverse as Otis Redding, Al Green, the Rolling Stones and Stevie Wonder, as well as many others, have recorded their own versions.

The Temptations' version was not only their first of four #1 pop hits but also the first of fifteen #1 hits on the R&B charts. With Ruffin's distinctive voice as lead, the group seemed to have found their sound at last, and his lead vocals would propel songs such as "Ain't Too Proud to Beg," "I Know I'm Losing You" and "Beauty Is Only Skin Deep" to chart success. But disagreements with Ruffin would eventually lead to him being fired from the group, and though the Temptations would continue to be successful, times were changing and the very nature of the songs changed. By the late 1960s, those feel-good, love-themed songs were few and far between.

While many songs that are now considered Carolina beach music classics were by regional groups or groups that didn't have a long string of hits on the charts, "My Girl" is one of those beach songs by a true supergroup. "My Girl," in turn, with its perfect beat and beach music–appropriate lyrics, has consequently become one of the all-time classics.

THE TRAMMPS

"HOLD BACK THE NIGHT"
1975, Billboard #35
Buddah 507

I t can be fairly hard to get a read on what type of group the legendary Trammps really were. Their first two releases in the 1970s, remakes of "Zing Went the Strings of My Heart" and "Sixty-Minute Man," were undisputed beach classics when done by the Coasters and the Dominoes, while their two biggest and highest-charting records, "Disco Inferno" and "That's Where the Happy People Go," are disco classics. Perhaps it's appropriate that their original beach music classic, "Hold Back the Night," might be seen as a bridge between both of their musical leanings.

The Philadelphia-based Trammps were originally formed as the Volcanos, and the group recorded a number of failed efforts between 1964 and 1966. They recorded another single as the Body Motions, and eventually elements of this group were formed into a new group by drummer and vocalist Earl Young. With new lead vocalist Jimmy Ellis, they performed as the Trammps, and Young was quoted as saying, "They were kind of raggedy when I first got them together, so the Trammps was a pretty appropriate name."

As the Trammps, they cut "Zing Went the Strings of my Heart" on Buddah in 1972, and as their first chart record it went to #64 on the pop charts and #17 on the R&B charts. Their next release, "Sixty-Minute Man," just bubbled under the Hot 100 at #108 in 1972, and despite the fact that a number of their subsequent singles made the R&B charts, only "Trusting Heart" (1974) made the pop charts, again just bubbling under at #101. Their

The Trammps. *Courtesy of Ed Cermanski.*

first Top 40 success came with "Hold Back the Night," the 1975 offering that came in at #35 and began the group's upward trajectory. The song was an obvious reworking of a B side instrumental called "Scrub Board" they had cut to back "Sixty-Minute Man" in 1972. With Jimmy Ellis singing a powerful lead, it not only broke into the U.S. Top 40, but like so many beach music hits, it was even better appreciated in England, where it moved into the Top 10.

As we now know, the group was just getting started, though subsequent tunes would be less soulful and more disco-based. From that point on, they would go to even greater fame, recording dozens of singles, including "That's Where the Happy People Go" (1976, #27) and their mega-hit "Disco Inferno." When first released, "Disco Inferno" only climbed to #53, but when rereleased in 1978, it shot to #11. Though these later Trammps efforts are clearly disco songs, they are so well crafted that even beach music fans can appreciate them.

The group continued into the '80s, but with the passing of disco it seemed that their moment, too, had passed. Nevertheless, the Trammps truly have been a group for the ages, as is their greatest beach music hit, "Hold Back the Night."

DORIS TROY

"JUST ONE LOOK"
1963, Billboard #10
Atlantic 2188

D oris Troy had an extensive musical pedigree, and during her career she would write for and work with luminaries such as Dee Clark, Jackie Wilson, Chuck Jackson, Solomon Burke, the Drifters, James Brown, George Harrison, Ringo Starr, Tom Jones, Steven Stills and many others. Despite all of this, she would chart only once, with her very first single for Atlantic, "Just One Look," a killer number that is a beach music favorite even today.

Born Doris Higgenson in New York City, she got her start in the music business working as an usher at the Apollo Theater in New York at age sixteen. Her first active role as a singer was as a part of a group known as the Halos, and she then recorded a solo side on Everest as Doris Payne (her grandmother's surname) in 1960. The single went nowhere, and she followed this with a duet with Doc Bagby on the Shirley label that same year, on a single as half of Jay and Dee on Arliss in 1961 and with Pearl Woods in the Gems on the Wall label in 1962.

All this time she was writing, however, and her song "How About That" had been a hit for Dee Clark in 1960. But it was when she recorded a demo of her own song, "Just One Look," in 1963 that everything changed. Atlantic loved the record so much that they released it straight off the demo she'd made without rerecording it. Somebody at Atlantic knew what they were doing, because it raced to #10 on the charts and became a bona fide hit.

Subsequent sides on Atlantic failed to find an American audience, though one of her Atlantic cuts, "Whatcha Gonna Do About It," made the British Top 40, and a number of her songs would be smashes in England as part of the Northern Soul scene. England would in fact show a greater appreciation for her talents than her homeland, and after frequent visits to the UK she eventually moved there in the late 1960s. In 1969, she signed with Apple records, which would allow her to work with Beatles Harrison and Starr, but she would never find further stateside success as a solo artist.

She cut a few singles into the 1970s, but even toward the end of her career as a solo artist, Troy was also doing session work as a background singer. She sang on a number of very famous recordings, including the Rolling Stones' "You Can't Always Get What You Want," and along with Clare Torry she provided the haunting backing vocals on the 1973 Pink Floyd album *Dark Side of the Moon*. Consequently, even though there are people who may not have heard the beach classic "Just One Look," countless millions have heard her efforts as a background singer—even if they didn't know who they were hearing.

THE TYMES

"SO MUCH IN LOVE"
1963, Billboard #1
Parkway 871

"MS. GRACE"
1974, Billboard #91
RCA 10128

M s. Grace' was just one of those records that took off," Tymes founder
Norm Burnett said in an interview for this book. "It went to #1 in
England, and even though it didn't chart as well here, we weren't disappointed.
Sure, we would have liked for it to have been a big record here, but we were
just happy it went to #1 there—it made us a really big act overseas. We
did a show with Stevie Wonder, and *we* were the featured act!" And when
"Ms. Grace" went to #1 in England, it meant that the Tymes accomplished
something no one else had ever done: along with 1963's "So Much in Love,"
they had #1 songs with two different records in two different countries in
two different decades, and neither song hit #1 in the other country. They
had also recorded two big beach music classics.

"We were named the Latineers because we thought the name sounded
good, like we had a Latin sound," Burnett told me. "About that time there
was a radio station contest for Tip Top bread. The deal was that you'd do
your song, they'd play it on the radio and people would send them the end
wrappers of the bread telling them who they liked in the contest. Well, we
were nervous, and we didn't sing our best. But a promoter heard our audition

The Tymes. *Courtesy of Norm Burnett.*

when we were doing our tape for the radio program, and he told us to go to Cameo-Parkway records and he gave us the number. We called and set up an audition with Billy Jackson, the A&R man."

For the audition, the group sang a song they had written called "As We Strolled," which would eventually be retitled "So Much in Love." "Well, a few weeks went by, and nobody called us, so we called them, and they were happy we called because they had lost the phone number!" Burnett said the group signed with Cameo-Parkway, but "Bernie Lowe, the owner of Cameo-Parkway, didn't like our name, so he named us the Tymes. I don't know where he got it, but that's how our name came about." With a new name, and a newly titled song, the group was hoping to get a little airplay but was in no way prepared for what was about to happen. They released "So Much in Love," and it went all the way to #1.

"We were young kids, just trying to make it, and money and stuff didn't interest us at that time," Burnett said. "But the song was bigger than us—we were really unprepared. We were on the label with Chubby Checker, Dee Dee Sharp, Bobby Rydell, the Orlons, the Dovells, and all of a sudden, 'So Much in Love' is a #1 record. We did a tour with Dick Clark, but our inexperience showed. Len Barry was with the Dovells at the time, and he came up and said, 'You guys perform like you just met right here on stage!' We really had to grow into the song."

"So Much in Love" kicked off a string of successful chart hits throughout the '60s, including "Wonderful! Wonderful!" (#7), but by the late '60s the gaps between hits were getting larger and the songs were charting lower, and it seemed that the group's time had passed. They were also singing backup for other artists, even providing the background vocals for old labelmate Len Barry on his #2 smash "1-2-3." But then they signed a deal with RCA and recorded some new songs, and the first released, "You Little Trustmaker," shot up to #12 on the Billboard charts. Suddenly, they were hot once again, and they followed that with the release of what many people consider the greatest all-time beach music classic, 1974's "Ms. Grace."

"Ms. Grace" was written by husband-and-wife team John and Johanna Hall (John would be a member of the group Orleans, which would later chart with hits such as "Still the One" and "Love Takes Time"), and despite the chart impetus provided by the success of "You Little Trustmaker, "Ms. Grace" only reached #91 on the Billboard charts. In England, however, it soared all the way to #1. "It's a nice song, a different type of song," Burnett says, "a really beautiful song." Yet surprisingly, the Tymes' newfound success was short-lived, and after charting once more, there were no more chart records.

As a result, the Tymes recorded two really big beach music hits at two different periods in their career. "So Much in Love" even opens with the sounds of the beach, but Burnett points out that it's just coincidental. "The surf and water sounds were added to the intro for something different. The O'Jays had 'Lonely Drifter' at about the same time—it was just a novelty thing." As for "Ms. Grace," it has played on thousands of jukeboxes and in thousands of clubs across the South and has emerged as what is arguably one of the greatest and most popular beach music songs of all time. Burnett says, "I'm really glad it is a big song on the Carolina beach music scene and that so many other acts like to sing it. I was in a club a few years back and heard a group playing it, and I said, 'That's a good song.' They said, 'Yeah, that's by the Tymes.' I said, 'Yeah, and I'm one of 'em!' 'Well,' they said, 'Give us the words, we've been singing the wrong words,' and so I did," Burnett laughed. "I'm just happy so many people like it." When it comes to "Ms. Grace," *like* may be an understatement.

BILLY WARD & THE DOMINOES

"Sixty-Minute Man"
1951, pre-Billboard
Federal 12022

Sixty-Minute Man" is not only a great beach record, but it's also considered one of the first real rock-and-roll records and also one of the first crossover records (a record by a black group that found popularity with both black and white listeners). Whether the record is beach, rock, rhythm and blues or anything else, it stands as one of the greatest classic songs of all time.

Billy Ward was raised playing the organ and was also trained in classical piano. After military service, he went to the Chicago Art Institute and the Julliard School of Music, and his career plans were to work as a vocal coach and Broadway arranger. While working as a Julliard instructor, Ward formed his own vocal group and enlisted students Clyde McPhatter, Charlie White, William Lamont and Bill Brown. Together they made up the Ques, who won some competitions at the Apollo Theater and on Arthur Godfrey's Talent Scouts Show in 1950. This caught the attention of King Records, and they convinced Ward that his group should try their hand at R&B. Soon Ward—who did the promotional work, wrote the songs and basically oversaw every aspect of the group now known as the Dominoes—had written several new songs, which the group recorded in 1950. Their first chart record was "Do Something for Me," which in 1951 went to #6 on the R&B charts, and though their next release did not do well, next came "Sixty-Minute Man"— and everything changed almost overnight.

Brown sang lead on "Sixty-Minute Man," and the double entendre lyrics and the song's rocking beat captured the ears of audiences everywhere. The song is about "Lovin' Dan," the "sixty-minute man" whose "fifteen minutes of teasin', fifteen minutes of squeezin and fifteen minutes of blowing [his] top" satisfies all the women. Because of the risqué nature of the song, it was banned by many radio stations, though some simply saw it as a novelty record. Today, many claim it was the first rock-and-roll record, though Ward himself wasn't sure what it was exactly. He said the song's distinctive sound came about almost by accident. DJ Charlie Brown provided the author with a sound clip on which Ward says that when he was first asked about that "rhythm and blues stuff, I didn't know what the heck [they were] talking about because I had a background in classical music. I wrote this song and we got a big laugh out of it. It was my attempt to write rhythm and blues I guess, but it didn't come out that way."

Whatever Ward was trying to do, it was a hit with listeners. "Sixty-Minute Man" was voted the year's #1 record in the jazz and blues field by music writers and by the national jukebox operators and was #1 on the R&B charts, where it was in the Top 10 for months. It even crossed over and hit #17 on the early pre-Billboard pop charts—a significant and almost unheard of accomplishment for a black group at the time. It also sold more than one million records, but perhaps most importantly, it bridged the gap between black music and white music, which was extremely significant not only in where pop music was at the time but in where beach music would later be as well.

All was not well within the group, however, and some members resented Ward's almost total control over most aspects of their lives. First White left the group, and then Brown left and formed the Checkers, where interestingly enough, he would reprise the role of Lovin' Dan on "Don't Stop Dan" in 1954. Dan's saga, where females tell him "Don't stop Dan, you have fifty-nine minutes to go!" didn't do much nationally, but other defectors would be more successful. After McPhatter sang lead on another big hit for the Dominoes, 1952's "Have Mercy Baby," he, too, decided to leave. Reportedly, McPhatter was disturbed that despite the fact that he was really the voice of the group—Ward himself only occasionally sang or played on their songs—he was a virtual unknown often passed off as Ward's younger brother. In early 1953, McPhatter left to form the Drifters, and he would later have a successful solo career as well.

Unlike many groups that crumbled after the defection of the lead singer, the Dominoes had another great talent waiting in the wings: Jackie Wilson. But despite the release of good records such as "Can't Do Sixty No More," the next entry in the "Lovin' Dan" saga, Dominoes records weren't selling. Eventually, Wilson also left—reportedly fired by Ward for "misconduct"—but he went on to have an obviously impressive solo career himself. The Dominoes would have several more Top 40 hits, but as the '50s wound down, the group's heyday was clearly behind them. There were frequent and numerous personnel changes in the ensuing years, and though Ward tried to keep the group together into the late '60s, by then they were relics of a bygone age. Nevertheless, "Sixty-Minute Man" was an important record not only in the annals of R&B and rock-and-roll but in beach music as well.

MARY WELLS

"MY GUY"
1964, Billboard #1
Motown 1056

"DEAR LOVER"
1966, Billboard #51
Atco 6392

Considering the body of great Motown hits churned out by Mary Wells in the 1960s, the odds are that any songs on this list would be those glitzy, Funk Brothers–backed classics from Detroit. And while one, her biggest hit "My Guy," *was* a Motown release, the other, "Dear Lover," is a post-Motown offering that oddly enough may have actually received far less publicity and airplay than it should have because of Wells's highly successful career with Motown—and her subsequent acrimonious relationship with Motown mogul Berry Gordy.

Mary Wells's career as a singer began well enough, and had things developed just a little differently, she might have been as much of a household name today as other Motown artists such as Stevie Wonder, Smokey Robinson and Diana Ross. That's not to say that she's unknown, and in fact, for a while she *was* a huge star and it looked like she might even go on to be Motown's biggest artist ever at one point. Her early songs, such as "The One Who Really Loves You" (#8), "You Beat Me to the Punch" (#9) and "Two Lovers" (#7), were all massive Top 10 hits, and three more Top 40 records followed. It was then that she recorded the Smokey Robinson–penned 1964 hit "My Guy," which went all the way to #1. Wells was for a brief moment the biggest Motown star of all. She toured with the Beatles, who unabashedly declared her to be their favorite American singer. Detroit, America and even England (she had been the first Motown star to perform there) seemed to be hers for the taking, and she was just turning twenty-one years old. And then things went very, very wrong.

There were apparently several issues that Wells thought were a problem at Motown. According to some sources, Wells didn't like the fact that Gordy was using her success to promote the Supremes (Marvin Gaye would later have the same suspicions about Diana Ross in regard to *his* career), and others said Wells was eager to break into movies and Motown wasn't moving in that direction. Accusation was followed by counteraccusation, and eventually, Wells left Motown by revealing that her contract with them had been signed when she was a seventeen-year-old minor. 20th Century Fox was there at the ready, however, and reportedly offered her as much as half a million dollars to sign with them, cut records and, to Wells's delight, make movies. Wells, it seemed, was poised for a new level of success.

Except that success did not come. She reportedly had a bit role in just one movie for 20th Century Fox, and only one of her records for Fox, 1965's "Use Your Head," broke the Top 40 at #34. In the meantime, Motown had cancelled her unreleased 1964 follow-ups to "My Guy"—and may have done more than just that. Wells's post-Motown failures were rumored to be due in part to Gordy, who allegedly asked DJs *not* to play her songs. Within a year she was out at Fox, taking with her but a small part of her massive contract earnings, and she then moved to Atco, where "Dear Lover" was her first, and most successful, single for that label—or any other label thereafter. It peaked at #51 in the Hot 100 and went all the way to #6 on the R&B charts, and both positions would be the highest her recordings would ever attain on either chart. Subsequently, she moved to Jubilee and then Epic, but after 1968 she'd never have a Top 100 record again.

Whether Wells was really a great talent wronged by big business or a prima donna who felt she wasn't getting her due and walked away, we may never know. But clearly "My Guy" was a song popular on every level that would later be recorded by many artists, including Aretha Franklin and the Supremes. The plaintive "Dear Lover" was the one gem to emerge from the shambles of a post-Motown career that arguably ended far too soon. Both are beach music classics.

MAURICE WILLIAMS
AND THE ZODIACS

"STAY"
1960, Billboard #1
Herald 552

"MAY I"
1965, did not chart
Dee-Su 304

Well-known Beach Music Hall of Fame DJ Charlie Brown said, "In my opinion the first beach music song was 'May I,' and I mean that in the sense that it was promoted *as* beach music. All they cared about was reaching the people of the Carolinas and Georgia, and that's what they wanted to do and they were happy with that. That, to me, is why 'May I' was such an important song." It would be hard to disagree with that assertion, and when you also consider that the group's song "Stay" was a big beach music and popular hit, and that Williams also wrote the doo-wop classic "Little Darlin'," it's clear that Maurice Williams was a musical genius. So if the idea was to market "May I" just as beach music, it was another stroke of genius by a master innovator.

Lancaster, South Carolina native Maurice Williams was interested in music from an early age. He first sang with the Junior Harmonizers, and by the age of thirteen he had formed his own band, which would eventually become the Gladiolas, consisting of Earl Gainey, William Massey, Norman Wade, Mac Badskins and Willie Jones. They realized Lancaster didn't offer the group a lot of opportunities, so eventually they went to Nashville to record a song Williams had written for Ernie Young's Excello records in Nashville in 1957. The song about a Lancaster girl Williams had dated was called "Little Darlin'" and did extremely well, reaching #41 on the charts. Soon Williams discovered that a white cover group, the Diamonds, wanted to do a version of the song. As he told Marion Carter, "At first I was against it, but Mr. Young gave me some very sound advice that I've always remembered: 'Don't let your ego get between you and your money. You wrote the song and the more copies you sell, the more money you make.'" He followed Young's advice, and when the cover version went all the way to #2 on the charts, it was apparent that Williams's good financial sense had served him well.

In 1958, the group left Excello, and because the Gladiolas name stayed with the label, they renamed themselves after an automobile called a Zodiac. They cut a few more singles and then the group dissolved. Later, Williams re-formed the Zodiacs with a new lineup, and their first big record as the Zodiacs was "Stay"—and it was big indeed. "Stay" was a song he had written years earlier about that same Lancaster girl and the night she had to leave because she had to be home by 10:00 p.m. He apparently didn't think as much of the song as he did the girl, however, and he told Carter, "I had never thought too much about 'Stay' and had thrown the lyrics in the trash. However, I still had a demo tape and one night we were playing demos and my girlfriend's sister heard it and went crazy over it. That changed my thinking, and we used the song as a demo for Al Silver at Herald Records."

In 1960, Herald released "Stay," and audiences loved hearing about Williams's efforts to persuade his girlfriend to remain past her curfew as he assures her that her parents won't mind if she stays for just one more dance. By November, the record had reached #1, and at one minute and thirty-seven seconds the record is well known for being at the shortest #1 record in the history of the Billboard charts. Today it's estimated that the record has sold more than ten million copies.

In 1965, Williams would release yet another classic hit, but whereas "Stay" had ridden its success to the top of the charts, "May I" wouldn't chart at all. Williams released "May I" on Vee Jay, but the label was in serious financial trouble and would in fact declare bankruptcy, and so Williams would rerelease the record on the New Orleans–based Dee-Su label. Though the record never charted, it was a favorite all along the East Coast and was so popular that Bill Deal and the Rhondels recorded it and had a Top 40 hit with it in 1969—mainly because everywhere they went people wanted to hear it. Amazingly, though "May I" never charted for the Zodiacs, it would sell over one million copies over the years and earn a gold record as well.

Maurice Williams is a success story in every way. A shrewd businessman, Williams told Ann Wicker in a 2008 interview, "I learned there was an awful lot of money in publishing—that's where the money really is. I started holding onto my own stuff...I was told to always hold onto my songs if I could." He did, and as a result Maurice Williams wrote—and, perhaps more importantly, kept the rights to—two of the biggest hits in beach music history, "Stay" and "May I." And they've been paying dividends ever since.

JACKIE WILSON

"(Your Love Keeps Lifting Me) Higher and Higher"
1967, Billboard #6
Brunswick 55336

There was perhaps no one more deserving of the moniker "Mr. Excitement" than Jackie Wilson. And while the name was given to him in reference to his dynamic on-stage performances, one would be hard-pressed not to see that his personal life was both lurid and tragic in ways that make the nickname doubly meaningful. Yet for all the controversy in his life, he recorded a number of songs now regarded as Carolina beach music classics, most particularly the Top 10 hit "Higher and Higher."

Jackie Wilson began singing at an early age, and though his first group, the Ever Ready Gospel Singers, sang religious tunes, Wilson's personal life was hardly the stuff of biblical exemplars. He was drinking by age nine, sent to a youth detention facility twice and frequently skipped school before dropping out altogether in the ninth grade. He tried his hand at boxing and then began singing professionally, first in a group and then as a solo act in nightclubs. He recorded his first single, "Danny Boy," as Sonny Wilson in 1952 and later joined Billy Ward and the Dominoes and stayed with them until 1957.

As a solo act, Wilson was fortunate to sign with Brunswick and work with songwriters Berry Gordy and Roquel Davis, who wrote a number of hits for Wilson, including "Reet Petite," "To Be Loved," "That's Why" and the Top 10 hit "Lonely Teardrops." After Gordy and Davis had a falling out with Wilson's manager, Nat Tarnopol, Wilson was without their songwriting genius, and as a result most of his early to mid-'60s recordings are less dynamic. This brought about a lull in his career, and from 1962 through 1965 he only charted once, with "Baby Workout."

His personal life, however, was going through anything but a lull. Though married, he was reputed to have been seeing a number of women, and one woman reported to be in a jealous rage shot him in 1961. Wilson had to have a kidney removed, another bullet was permanently lodged near his spine and he was in the hospital for a month and a half (to this day, the story that she was a crazed fan, and not a spurned lover, continues to circulate). He was also out of money (despite reportedly making roughly $250,000 a year by this point), and his wife divorced him in 1965. In 1967, he and a friend were arrested on moral charges in South Carolina after being discovered in a motel with two twenty-four-year-old white women. But just as it appeared Wilson was about to become more famous for making the tabloids than hit records, he started working with producer Carl Davis (who had also produced Mary Wells's "Dear Lover"), and his career was rejuvenated. Under Davis's tutelage, in 1966 he recorded "Whispers," which went to #11, and then the legendary "(Your Love Keeps Lifting Me) Higher and Higher." For "Higher and Higher," Davis had Motown's legendary Funk Brothers play the backing tracks in Chicago, and Wilson added his vocals in New York. In an interview with Bill Dahl, Davis said, "I remember I brought the track into New York. And we went into the studio, and Jackie started singing it, and it was completely different from what I thought it should sound like. And I told him, 'No, no, no, no. I don't like that.' He told me, 'Well, come out here and sing it how you want it sung!' So I came out and I told him, 'This is the way it needs to go.' He said, 'Oh, that's what you want?' I said, 'Yeah.' He went back in there and in one take he did it."

Davis apparently knew the magic formula, because the song went to #1 on the R&B charts and #6 on the Top 40. The song would actually chart three times in England, hitting #11 in 1969, #25 in 1975 and #15 in 1987. Ultimately, the record would reach four million in sales and would be named to *Rolling Stone*'s list of "The 500 Greatest Songs of All Time."

Wilson followed "Higher and Higher" with another twenty-plus singles, including the Davis-produced 1968 beach favorite, "I Get the Sweetest Feeling." Living up to his Mr. Excitement nickname until the end, he had a heart attack on stage during a performance in 1975 and remained in a semi-comatose state for the rest of his life before passing away in 1984 at the age of forty-nine.

Certainly there was nothing boring about Jackie Wilson's life or his music, and in that sense the high-energy "Higher and Higher" is the perfect song to represent his legacy for beach music lovers everywhere.

BRENTON WOOD

"THE OOGUM BOOGUM SONG"
1967, Billboard #34
Double Shot 111

"GIMME LITTLE SIGN"
1967, Billboard #9
Double Shot 116

"The Oogum Boogum Song' was a sign of the times," Brenton Wood told me in an interview for this book. "Miniskirts and bellbottom pants were all the new fashions of the sixties. And it was a song that I really enjoyed writing." His follow-up, "Gimme Little Sign," was less a sign of the times and more about his own personal issues with a girlfriend. Both tunes struck a chord with listeners in 1967 and are songs beach music lovers consider classics as well.

Brenton Wood was born Alfred Jesse Smith in Shreveport, Louisiana, before his family moved to California, where after high school he attended Compton College. An accomplished piano player, he had already dabbled in singing as a member of the Dootones under his real name. He soon changed his name to Brenton Wood and sang under that for the first time as a member of the Quotations at Compton and next as a member of Little Freddy & the Rockets, who recorded "All My Love" on the Chief label in 1958. Over the next few years, he cut a number of singles on different labels, including "The Kangaroo" (1960), "Mr. Schemer" (1963) and others.

Brenton Wood. *Courtesy of Brenton Wood.*

Just when it appeared that Wood was a talented singer who couldn't find a market, he signed with Double Shot records in 1967. His first recording for the label would become "The Oogum Boogum Song," but it took some work to get it where it ended up. Wood said that initially the song had a very different sound and feel—and didn't have the "Oogum Boogum" hook. "The record company gave me a song one day called 'Casting My Spell on You.' I didn't like it very much, so I took the song and rewrote it and added the hook 'Oogum Boogum,' which is another word for abracadabra. It took me six weeks, but I laughed all through it. It was a joy."

Listeners found "Oogum Boogum" to be a joy as well. It reached #19 on the R&B charts and #34 on the Billboard Hot 100, so the expectations were high for his next recording. That single was "Gimme Little Sign," and Wood said, "'Gimme Little Sign' came to me after a few breakups with my girlfriend" and is his plaintive plea for his girl to give him some sign that things weren't as they should be. The catchy tune, which at no point in its lyrics ever actually says "gimme little sign"—it's always "gimme *some kind of* sign"—raced to #9 on the Billboard charts and #19 on the R&B charts in 1967. After two big hits, it looked like Brenton Wood and Double Shot were a successful combination.

After "Gimme Little Sign," his next 1967 release, "Baby You Got It," peaked at #34 in November, but despite the slight drop-off after the popularity of "Gimme Little Sign," the string of three consecutive Top

40 songs gave hope for a promising future. But his next single, "Lovey Dovey Kinda Lovin'," failed to make the Top 40, peaking at #99 in March 1968. This was the beginning of a trend, as his next release, "Me and You" (1968) would bubble under the Hot 100 at #121, his next wouldn't chart at all and his next, "A Change Is Gonna Come" (1969), would also bubble under at #131. Unfortunately, that was Brenton Wood's last single to make the Billboard pop charts, as subsequent singles on Double Shot all stiffed.

Wood continued to record throughout the '70s on a variety of labels, but other than his 1977 cover of the Fleetwoods' 1959 hit "Come Softly to Me," which barely entered the bottom of the R&B charts, he never charted after 1969. To this day, however, he appreciates what beach music is and how it keeps his music alive. "'Oogum Boogum' and 'Gimme Little Sign' were two of my best works," he says, "so it is an honor to be recognized for something you enjoy so much. I played North and South Carolina back in the '70s and always appreciated you all for your awareness of my music." Beach music lovers would say the honor is all theirs.

WORKS CITED

Abrahamian, Bob. E-mails to author. July 15 and 23 and August 13, 2010.

———. "Sitting in the Park." www.sittinginthepark.com/index.html.

Baker, Mike. "Mike Baker and the Forgotten 45s." web.me.com/mikebaker/themob/themob.html.

Benicewitz, Larry. "Remembering Willie Tee." *The Blues Art Journal* (November 2007). www.bluesart.at/NeueSeiten/REMEMBERING%20WILLIE%20TEE%20(1944-2007).html.

"Benny Spellman." Louisiana Music Hall of Fame. louisianamusichalloffame.org.

"Black Bubblegum." *Bubblegum University.* www.bubblegum-music.com/blackbubblegum.

Bogdanov, Vladimir. *All Music Guide to Soul: The Definitive Guide to R&B and Soul.* N.p.: Backbeat Books, 2003.

Bounden, Stephen. "Maurice Williams: A Brief History of This American Singer and Songwriter." SoulMotion. www.soulmotion.co.uk/Maurice%20Williams.htm.

Bradley, Jan. Telephone interview with the author. August 15, 2010.

"Brenton Wood's Biography." www.brentonwood.com/html/biography.html.

Brewster, Bill, and Frank Broughton. *Last Night a DJ Saved My Life*. New York: Grove Press, 2000.

Bronson, Fred. *The Billboard Book of Number One Hits*. N.p.: Billboard, 1988.

Broven, John. *Rhythm and Blues in New Orleans*. Gretna, LA: Pelican, 1978.

———. *South to Louisiana: The Music of the Cajun Bayous*. Gretna, LA: Pelican, 1983.

Burnett, Norm. Telephone interview with the author. December 20, 2010.

Cameron, G.C. Telephone interview with the author. February 4, 2011.

Cermanski, Edward. "The Trammps." E-mails to author. April 15 and 16, 2010.

Channel, Bruce. "Hey! Baby." E-mails to author. August 23, December 19, 2010.

Craver, Paul. "Cannonball." E-mails to author. June 8 and 9, August 1, 2010.

Curry, Clifford. Telephone interview with the author, October 31, 2010, February 2, 2011.

Curtis, Clem. "The Foundations." E-mails to author. June 8, 9 and 15, 2010.

Dahl, Bill. "Jackie Wilson." Brunswick Records. www.brunswickrecords. com/artists/jackiewilson.htm.

Deville, Hershey. Telephone interview with the author, November 19, 2010.

Freeland, David. *The Ladies of Soul*. Oxford: University Press of Mississippi, 2001.

Gardner, Veta, and Earl Gardner. E-mails to author. July 14 and August 13, 2010.

Haynes, Greg. *The Heeey Baby Days of Beach Music*. N.p., 2005.

Hobson, Donald. "I Need a Love." E-mails to author. September 7, October 18 and 19, November 10 and 15, 2010; February 3, 2011.

Holvay, James. E-mails to author. September 30 and October 2, 9 and 7, 2010.

"Interview with Richard Younger. Get a Shot of Rhythm and Blues: The Arthur Alexander Story." www.allbutforgottenoldies.net/interviews/richard-younger.

"Jackie Wilson." The History of Rock. www.history-of-rock.com/jackie_wilson.htm.

James, Linda "Quig" Quinlan. "Hey I Know You." E-mails to author. June 29 and 30, July 1, 2, 9, 10 and 13, 2010; January 30, 2011.

Jancik, Wayne. *The Billboard Book of One-Hit Wonders*. New York: Billboard Books, 1990.

Kaye, Candy. "The Spiral Starecase." E-mail to author. April 14, 2010.

Kilgour, Colin. "Gene McDaniels." Black Cat Rockabilly. www.rockabilly.nl/references/messages/gene_mcdaniels.htm.

Kuban, Bob. Telephone interview with the author. August 23, 2010.

Lemon, Meadowlark. Telephone interview with the author. January 11, 2011.

Lewis, Pete. "The Four Tops: B&S Classic Interview." B&S Online. www.bluesandsoul.com/feature/357/the_four_tops_bands_classic_interview.

Lewsiohn, Mark. *The Beatles Recording Sessions*. New York: Hyperion, 1992.

Lollar, Sam. "Jewell and the Rubies." E-mails to author. April 18, 19 and 20, 2010.

Marsh, Dave. *The Heart of Rock & Soul: The 1001 Greatest Singles Ever Made.* New York: Da Capo Press, 1999.

McDaniels, Gene. Telephone interview with the author. November 15, 2010.

McElrath, John. "The Medallions.com." www.medallions.com/index5F/ history.html.

———. Telephone interview with the author. July 19, 2010.

Millar, Bill. "Arthur Alexander." The Alabama Music Hall of Fame Website. www.alamhof.org/arthuralexander.html.

Moore, Bobby, Jr. Telephone interview with the author. November 1, 2010.

Moore, Deacon John. Telephone interview with the author. November 19, 2010.

Newsom, Jim. "Beach Music's Five Star General." www. generalnormanjohnson.com.

———. "Who Put the 'H' in Rhondel?" http://jimnewsom.com/PFW-Billdeal.html.

Parker, Steve. "The Northern Soul Top 500." Steve Parker Micro Site. www. rocklistmusic.co.uk/steveparker/northern_soul_top_500.htm.

Payne, Freda. Telephone interview with the author. February 5, 2011.

Peoples Bears, Sandra. Telephone interview with the author. November 20, 2010.

Perrone, Pierre. "Bobby Moore: Leader of the Rhythm Aces." *The Independent,* March 18, 2006. www.independent.co.uk/news/obituaries/ bobby-moore-470305.html.

———. "Earl Nelson: Half of Bob and Earl." *The Independent.* www. independent.co.uk/news/obituaries/earl-nelson-half-of-bob-earl-880270.htm.

Pittman, Wayne. Telephone interview with the author. November 3, 2010.

Pope, Dianne, and Charles Pope. E-mails to author. June 25, July 11 and August 23, 25, 27 and 28, 2010.

Pruter, Robert. *Chicago Soul*. Chicago: University of Illinois Press, 1991.

Rachou, David. "Jewel and the Rubies." E-mail to author. April 20, 2010.

Roberts, Kev. *The Northern Soul Top 500*. London: Bee Cool Publishing, 2003.

"Sad Eyes." superseventies.com/sw_sadeyes.html.

Scott, Billy. E-mails to the author. November 10, 2010; January 30, 2011.

———. Telephone interview with the author. November 1, 2010.

"Soulful Kinda Music." www.soulfulkindamusic.net/discographies.htm.

"Spiral Starecase." Mclane & Wong Entertainment Law. www.benmclane. com/spiral.htm.

Tharp, Ammon. Telephone interview with the author. November 10, 2010.

"Those Hoodlum Friends: The Coasters." www.angelfire.com/mn/coasters.

Threatt, Sonny. "Sunny and Phyllis." E-mails to author. May 27, 28, 29 and 30 and August 16, 2010.

Tomlinson, Bobby. Telephone interview with the author. August 1, 2010.

Turner, Sonny. Telephone interview with the author. August 10, 2010.

Upton, Pat. "More Today." E-mails to author. June 10 and October 19, 2010.

Washburn, Mark Lawrence Toppmann, and April Baker. "Beach Music Icon General Johnson Dies." *Charlotte Observer*, October 15, 2010. www. charlotteobserver.com/2010/10/15/1761650/beach-music-icon-general-johnson.html.

Webb, Robert. "Double Take: 'Hold Back the Night' The Trammps / Graham Parker and the Rumour." *The Independent.* www.independent. co.uk/arts-entertainment/music/features/double-take-hold-back-the-night-the-trammps--graham-parker-and-the-rumour-592563.html.

Weiss, Ed. Telephone interview with the author. August 12, 2010.

Whitburn, Joel. *The Billboard Book of Top 40 Hits.* New York: Billboard Publications, 1996.

———. *Top Pop Singles, 1955–1986.* Menomonee Falls, WS: Record Research, 1987.

Wicker, Ann. *Making Notes: Music of the Carolinas.* Charlotte, NC: Novello Festival Press, 2008.

Wood, Brenton. "Brenton Wood Information." E-mails to author. May 5 and October 18, 2010.

Younger, Richard. E-mails to author. October 31 and December 19, 2010.

———. *Get a Shot of Rhythm and Blues: The Arthur Alexander Story.* Tuscalooosa: University of Alabama Press, 2000.

———. "The Life and Times of Arthur Alexander." www.richardyounger. com/arthur-alexander.php.

ABOUT THE AUTHOR

D r. Rick Simmons was born and raised in South Carolina, and during the course of his education, he attended Clemson University, Coastal Carolina University and the University of South Carolina, where he completed his PhD in 1997. He currently lives in Louisiana with his wife, Sue, and his children, Courtenay and Cord, though he still spends a portion of the summer at his family home in Pawleys Island, South Carolina. He is the holder of the George K. Anding Endowed Professorship at Louisiana Tech University, where he is currently the director of the Honors Program and the Center for Academic and Professional Development. This is his fourth book, and two of his previous books, *Hidden History of the Grand Strand* (2010) and *Defending South Carolina's Coast: The Civil War from Georgetown to Little River* (2009), were also published by The History Press.

Visit us at
www.historypress.net